Getting Behavioral Interventions Right

Proper Uses to Avoid Common Abuses

D1308079

Beverley H. Johns

Publications

LRP Publications
Horsham, Pennsylvania 19044

This publication was designed to provide accurate and authoritative information in regard to the subject matter covered. It is published with the understanding that neither the author nor the publisher is engaged in rendering legal, accounting, or other professional service. If legal advice or other expert assistance is required, the service of a competent professional should be sought.

Library of Congress Cataloging-in-Publication Data

Johns, Beverley H. (Beverley Holden)
    Getting behavioral interventions right : proper uses to avoid common abuses / Beverley H. Johns.
      p.   cm.
    Includes bibliographical references.
    ISBN 1-57834-048-9
    1. Problem children--Education--United States. 2. Problem children--Behavior modification--United States. 3. Behavior disorders in children. I. Title.

LC4802.J65   2005
371.93--dc22

                                  2005040840

About the Author

BEVERLEY HOLDEN JOHNS has 35 years of experience working with students with learning disabilities and students with severe behavioral disorders in the public schools of Illinois. She was the founder and the administrator of the Garrison Alternative School for students with severe behavioral disorders in Jacksonville, Ill., and was the coordinator of staff development for the Four Rivers Special Education District. She is now a learning and behavior consultant and also an adjunct instructor for MacMurray College in Jacksonville.

Ms. Johns is the lead author of five books, including LRP Publications' *Students with Disabilities & General Education: A Desktop Reference for School Personnel, Reduction of School Violence: Alternatives to Suspension, Third Edition*, and a workbook for a video titled, *The Paraprofessional's Guide to Managing Student Behavior*. The other books she has written cover the topics of managing verbally and physically aggressive students, safe schools, and effective curriculum and instruction for students with emotional/behavioral disorders. She is also the lead author of a monograph on "Successful Inclusion of E/BD Students," and an article on "Leadership in Special Education." Ms. Johns has also presented workshops across the United States and abroad.

Ms. Johns is the recipient of the 2000 CEC Outstanding Leadership Award from the International Council for Exceptional Children and past international president of the Council for Children with Behavioral Disorders. She is listed in *Who's Who in America, Who's Who of American Women*, and *Who's Who in American Education*. She has served as chair of governmental relations for several national and state organizations concerned with the needs of both regular and general educators and exceptional children.

She is immediate past president of the Learning Disabilities Association of Illinois and has served as that organization's national state presidents' representative on the national board of LDA of America. And Ms. Johns was Jacksonville Woman of the Year in 1988 and cochaired the Business Education Partnership Committee and the Jacksonville Truancy Task Force.

Ms. Johns is a graduate of Catherine Spalding College in Louisville, Ky., and received a fellowship for her graduate work where she earned a master's degree in special education at Southern Illinois University in Carbondale. She has done post-graduate work at the University of Illinois, Western Illinois University, SIU, and Eastern Illinois University.

Table of Contents

Introduction

"I tried that and it didn't work" is a common complaint regarding certain behavioral interventions. Here's the typical scenario: A student is exhibiting a behavior problem. A team of people meets to create a behavioral intervention plan or a Section 504 plan, or the team provides intervention guidance to a teacher who is struggling with an at-risk student. Ultimately, the team recommends an intervention. It doesn't work. School personnel respond negatively because they don't understand the integrity of the intervention or they have used the intervention incorrectly and lost faith in it.

Getting Behavioral Interventions Right: Proper Uses to Avoid Common Abuses is designed to provide a better understanding of 18 common behavioral interventions used in today's schools. Each segment focuses on providing examples of appropriate and inappropriate uses of a specific intervention, a definition of the intervention, how to assure that the intervention is implemented correctly, and cautions when using the intervention.

Your goal while using any behavioral intervention must be to do no harm to children and to change behavior positively. Ill-conceived or poorly implemented behavioral interventions do not result in long-term behavior change. Instead, they foster fear and anger in children, while also setting a negative example for the students we serve.

For several months leading up to the publication of this book, subscribers to LRP Publications' subscriber-based Web site, *Special Ed Connection* (*www.specialedconnection.com*), were invited to submit interventions for which they needed help or were seeking more information. A limited number of some of these "problem interventions" were selected for discussion on the Web site or via e-mail with the author, and later became part of this book.

It is not the intent of the series to discuss, endorse or critique any commercially designed products; rather, the focus is on specific methods commonly used in today's schools.

Intervention #1 - Time-Out

Scenarios

Imagine these common scenarios in a school.

Appropriate Use of Time-Out – Scenario #1

Billy and Melissa, first-graders, are tossing a ball back and forth. The teacher, Mrs. Jones, notices that Melissa takes the ball and throws it as hard as she can at Billy so he can't catch it. Mrs. Jones responds by saying to Melissa: "I need you to throw the ball to Billy so Billy can catch it, or I am going to have to take it away from you."

Mrs. Jones then shows Melissa how to throw the ball appropriately. Melissa just looks at Mrs. Jones and deliberately throws the ball as hard as ever at Billy. Mrs. Jones then takes the ball away from Melissa and tells her she cannot play with it for the next five minutes.

Mrs. Jones proceeds to play ball with Billy, while Melissa has to sit by herself and watch. Mrs. Jones praises Billy for throwing the ball appropriately. She ignores Melissa. In five minutes, she tells Melissa that she can now play ball with Billy if she can throw it appropriately. Melissa returns to play ball and throws it appropriately. Mrs. Jones praises her for throwing the ball correctly.

Mrs. Jones used a form of time-out that we will discuss. She provided a warning to Melissa. Melissa continued the inappropriate behavior. Mrs. Jones then did what she said she would do — remove the ball from Melissa and make her sit in a designated area where she could still see the activity but could not participate. Mrs. Jones ignored Melissa during that period of time but still could see what Melissa was doing. Mrs. Jones then modeled the appropriate way to throw the ball and praised Bill for his appropriate behavior. When the designated time was up, Melissa came back to the activity, and when she engaged in appropriate behavior, Mrs. Jones praised her.

Appropriate Use of Time-Out – Scenario #2

In another classroom, Mrs. Bryant is a seventh-grade English teacher with 24 students. She has provided directions to her students for a

1

written assignment. Jeremy yells out that he isn't going to do that "f___ing paper."

Mrs. Bryant walks over to Jeremy and states in a quiet and calm voice: "Swearing is not allowed in this classroom; I need you to start your assignment. If you do not start the assignment, I will need you to go to time-out." Jeremy yells again; this time louder than the first time. Mrs. Bryant states: "Jeremy, I need you to go to time-out — I can either buzz the office that you will come on your own and have someone meet you right outside this classroom, or I will get assistance to escort you. It's your choice. I know you can make a good decision for yourself."

Jeremy says that he will walk, and Mrs. Bryant buzzes the office for someone to come to the classroom door. The assistant principal, Mr. Larson, comes to the door and walks Jeremy to time-out. The time-out room is a separate room with no door and nothing in it. Jeremy enters the room. Mr. Larson stands outside the room and says to Jeremy: "Jeremy, I need you to ask me to start your time." Jeremy replies to start his time. Mr. Larson says: "Thank you — I will start your time."

Mr. Larson turns away from Jeremy, looks at his watch, and times five minutes. Jeremy stands quietly for five minutes while Mr. Larson says nothing to him. When the five-minute time-out period is over, Mr. Larson talks with Jeremy briefly to prepare him for his return to the classroom. Mr. Larson discusses the following questions: What happened? What did you do? What could you do if this happens again?

Mr. Larson then asks Jeremy to tell him what he will do when he returns to the classroom. Jeremy replies that he will do his work. Mr. Larson provides him with a word of confidence and says: "I know you can do that and do the assignment well." Mr. Larson walks Jeremy back to the classroom. Jeremy goes to his desk and starts working on his assignment. After a short period of time, Mrs. Bryant goes over to Jeremy to see if he has any questions or whether she can provide him with assistance.

Mrs. Bryant used seclusion time-out. Jeremy was being disruptive. She gave Jeremy a warning and also provided choices. She then called for assistance. Mr. Larson knew how to appropriately use time-

out and did so. He then returned Jeremy to the classroom where Jeremy received positive reinforcement from Mrs. Bryant when he was working appropriately.

The above were two examples of the appropriate use of time-out. Now picture these scenarios:

Inappropriate Use of Time-Out

1. Mrs. Krell sends Jason to the school's time-out room adjacent to the principal's office. He takes his work there and remains in the room the rest of the day where he can be supervised by the school secretary (along with her many other duties), and where he also can hear all of the activities taking place in the office.

2. Mr. Meeks has sent Melissa to the time-out room, which is a separate room in the school. A staff member stands outside the room to supervise Melissa. As people pass the staff member standing outside the room, they stop and chat with him.

3. Mrs. Jacobs puts Bill, along with his desk, out in the hall and says she is using time-out.

4. Mr. Gray sends Alex home for the rest of the day and calls it time-out.

These obviously are incorrect uses of time-out and will result in an ineffective intervention for making positive changes in behavior. Throughout the country these instances occur daily because some individuals do not understand the correct use of this intervention.

Let's now look at the definition of time-out, how to use it correctly, and cautions in its use.

Definition of Time-Out

Sulzer and Mayer (1972) defined time-out as: ". . . a process through which access to the sources of reinforcement are removed for a particular time period contingent upon the emission of a response." (p. 154). It is the removal of any opportunity to receive reinforcement. The student is receiving no attention, positive or negative, during the time-out. It involves ignoring the student for a period of time. It makes the assumption that the student will receive no reinforcement during the period of the time-out.

Many years ago in the classroom, I can remember removing a student with autism to the designated time-out area and he began masturbating — obviously this was not time-out for this particular student. It also makes the assumption that the time-in area from which the child was removed is indeed reinforcing. In order for time-out to work, the area *from which the child has been removed* must be a place where the child really wants to be. Careful consideration must be given to whether the classroom is reinforcing to the child or whether the child is going to time-out to avoid the classroom.

There are two types of time-out. "Nonexclusionary time-out" involves removing reinforcers from the student without changing the student's physical location. As an example, the teacher might have the student place his head down on the desk for a short period of time, or the teacher might decide to ignore the student. It should be noted that aggressive behavior should not be ignored. Low-level aggression ignored will turn into high-level aggression, because the student perceives that the teacher is doing nothing and therefore condones the behavior. Another example of nonexclusionary time-out would include removing a favored object from the child.

It may be very difficult to utilize time-out within the classroom, because while the teacher might decide to ignore a student, the other students might reinforce the student in time-out. When I was using a nonexclusionary time-out of ignoring a student for inappropriate behavior, I taught the other students that they were not to pay attention to students who were engaging in inappropriate behavior, and I reinforced them for working on the task at hand rather than attending to the student who was acting up.

"Exclusionary time-out" involves removing the student from the time-in environment. By removing the student from the classroom, you are using a more intrusive and restrictive intervention. Johns et al. (1996) outline three major types of exclusionary time-out: contingent observation, exclusion, and isolation/seclusion. In contingent observation, the student is removed to another location in the classroom, playground or cafeteria and instructed to watch but not participate in the activities. Exclusion time-out means the student is removed from the instructional activities and is not able to watch the classroom activities. Isolation/seclusion requires the student to leave the class-room and enter a separate time-out room for a brief period of time.

Correct Use of Time-Out

If used effectively, time-out can be a very effective behavioral intervention, but it is indeed one of the most abused behavioral interventions. It must be used in conjunction with positive reinforcement for the opposite appropriate behavior. As an example, the student has been sent to a separate area outside the classroom for swearing at the teacher. When the student is engaging in appropriate language, then it is critical that the teacher provides positive verbal reinforcement to the student.

Time-out is the opportunity for the student to regain control. During the short amount of time when no one is talking with the student and the student is not doing anything, the student has the time to stand quietly and regain his/her composure. A short amount of time can be defined as a period not to exceed five minutes. For younger students or for those who have significant cognitive disabilities, a shorter amount of time is suggested. The student should remain quiet for that period of time.

➤ **When the student is yelling or screaming during time out**

If the child is yelling and screaming, the time should not be started. Usually if the student is being ignored, he or she will quiet down. However, if the student refuses to quiet down and continues to scream, here are some possible strategies I've found to be effective.

1. If the student settles down and is quiet for even 30 seconds, the adult can say: "Thank you for being quiet. I will now start your time."

2. If the student continues to yell, and it doesn't appear that he/she is going to quiet down for a period of time, the adult can say: "I will give you one minute to quietly ask to start your time, then I will start 'time for time' and take time from your recess." For older students, you may want to take time from their lunch period or another free period. Or, "time for time" may mean that the student has to make up the time after school. This will

depend on your school's policies and procedures and should be worked out ahead of time. I have found this strategy very effective for students with the most significant behavioral problems.

3. A third strategy that I have used when a student is yelling, calling out names and making statements like, "My lawyer will get you fired," is to tell the student: "If you continue to yell, I am going to have to tape your comments." This usually results in the student quieting down. If you are considering this procedure, your school should have a policy that provides for the use of audio or video taping of the student. This also should be discussed during the development of the student's behavioral intervention plan. Such tapes do become part of the student's record. I will never tape a student unless I have given notice that I am going to do so.

➤ Ignoring the student

Time-out also only works if the adult is truly ignoring the student, whether the student is removed from the classroom or the student is ignored within the classroom. In some of the examples of inappropriate use of time-out, the adult is paying attention to the student. This can become attention-getting for the student and therefore defeats the effectiveness of the time-out strategy.

When the adult decides to use time-out, the adult must not talk to the student or attend to the student's behavior in any way for a short period of time — usually not to exceed five minutes of quiet behavior. The student is also not allowed to do work or talk during the time-out period.

And the student must be supervised at all times. For time-out to be most effective, the adult should not be directly looking at the student and should be standing away from the child. However, the student should be within the adult's view.

➤ Time-out in the behavioral intervention plan

If the IEP team determines time-out to be an effective intervention for an individual student, its use should be delineated as part of the behavioral intervention plan.

6

➢ Create a written report

Create a written report each time a seclusion time-out is used. The documentation should include, at a minimum, the time at which the student was placed in time-out, the time the student left, the behavior exhibited that resulted in the time-out, the behavior during the time-out, and the person(s) who supervised the time-out. The written report becomes part of the student's temporary record. State law and regulations may require that the report be sent to the parent.

➢ Too much time-out?

If time-out procedures are being used too often with a student, the team must look at whether it is appropriate for the child. The following are some questions the IEP team might ask:

1. Is the student utilizing time-out in order to get out of class?

2. Is the student in the time-out room receiving no reinforcement?

3. Is the person supervising the student refraining from talking to the student during the time-out?

➢ Time-out as policy

Any school district that uses an exclusionary time-out should develop policies and procedures on its use, and the policies should be disseminated to parents and families. Teachers also should be provided adequate training in the use of the procedures.

➢ Tips for seclusion time-out

Seclusion time-out in a separate time-out room outside the classroom should be used only as a last resort, after other management techniques have failed and the student still continues to disrupt the classroom. If a separate room is going to be used, the following requirements should apply (some states may have additional requirements):

1. The room should meet life safety codes and be constructed of materials acceptable to meet those codes.

2. The room should be free of objects and fixtures with which a child could cause self-injury.

3. The room should be properly lighted and ventilated.

4. The room should not be in a high traffic area of the school if at all possible. If a student has lost control, it is embarrassing for the student to be seen by other students. Likewise, the student may decide to "put on a show" for other students.

5. There should be a means by which an adult can continuously monitor, by sight and sound, the student's behavior. Children must be supervised at all times.

6. There should be no door, or if there is one, it should be unlocked. Some states do have provisions for locking the door. Locking the door should be done with great caution; locking some students in a room may traumatize them. However, "[f]or the most part, the use of locked time-out room does not appear to offend the federal Constitution or otherwise violate federal law." (See SmartStart: Time-Out, *Special Ed Connection*™, LRP Publications.)

7. The floor area of the room should be at least 4 feet by 4 feet and the ceiling at least seven feet high, floor to ceiling. A school district I knew wanted to build a time-out room within another room and decided that the time-out room did not need a ceiling. One of the first times they used the room, the student climbed out over the wall. Another student threw items of clothing over the top of the wall.

When using a seclusion time-out, use the following steps to assure its appropriate use:

1. When the child comes to the time-out room and is quiet, the child should ask the adult to start his or her time: "Please start my time." The adult should thank the child for being calm and say in a very quiet tone of voice: "Thank you, yes I will start your time." It is important that the student make the

request appropriately. If the student yells to start his time, the adult quietly says: "I will be happy to start your time when you ask quietly." Once I had a staff member who was working with a child with mental retardation and the staff member said to the student, "Nancy, you need to ask in a sentence to start your time." Nancy looked up at the staff member and said, "Please start my time in a sentence."

2. The adult then starts the predetermined time. The child is expected to remain quiet. If the child does not do so, the time starts over.

3. When the time is over, the adult should talk with the student to process the event that resulted in the time-out. I use questions like: "Tell me what happened." "What did you do?" "What could you do the next time this happens?" This is the teachable moment — an opportunity to use a negative event that resulted in the child being in time-out as an opportunity to talk with the child about other options he or she has if such a situation happens again. (Johns 2002).

4. After the processing of the event is complete, the adult should provide encouragement to the student. "I know you can have a good rest of the day." The adult always wants to leave the child on a positive note, showing that the adult has faith that the student can do well. The adult might also have the student verbalize what kind of day he is going to have for the remainder of the day. If the student says he will have a good rest of the day, then he is more likely to have one.

➤ Post your time-out rules

Johns and Carr (2002) have recommended a set of rules that should be established and posted in the time-out room area. The rules include:

1. Students will refrain from talking to anyone outside the time-out room.

2. Students will refrain from touching light switches.

3. Students will stand away from the doorway or wherever the staff member indicates.

4. Students will sit or stand during the time-out. Students will refrain from sleeping.

5. Students will refrain from taking objects into the time-out room. If the student throws any object, it will be held until the end of the day.

An 8th Circuit Court case in 2003 (*CJN by SKN v. Minneapolis Pub. Schs.*, 38 IDELR 208) addressed the use of extended time-outs to control the behavior of a third-grader. The court determined that the IEP was reasonably calculated to provide the student, CJN, with educational benefit. In this case, CJN did make academic progress and the school had acted in good faith. The school also provided positive reinforcement for appropriate behavior. (*The Special Education 2004 Desk Book*, LRP Publications, 2004; "Year to Date: Top behavior-related cases of 2003," *Special Ed Connection*™, July 28, 2003.)

Cautions in the Use of Time-Out

1. Check within your own state to see whether there are specific laws and regulations that govern the use of time-out and follow them.

2. Before using time-out, make sure policies and procedures have been developed and adopted.

3. When using time-out with a student receiving special education, make sure it is outlined within the student's behavioral intervention plan, along with procedures for the use of positive reinforcement for appropriate behavior and procedures for teaching appropriate behaviors.

4. Time-out could be considered an unreasonable seizure in violation of the Fourth Amendment if it wasn't justified at inception and reasonable in its scope. Courts have considered these factors: the nature of the misconduct, location of the time-out room, size of the time-out room, interior of the time-out room, safety considerations, amount of isolation, amount of time spent in time-out, how time is spent during time-out,

and district policy. (SmartStart: Time-Out, *Special Ed Connection*™, LRP Publications.)

5. Make sure seclusion time-out is not contraindicated for psychological or physical health reasons. (SmartStart: Time-Out, *Special Ed Connection*™, LRP Publications.)

6. Time-out is not an area where the student has access to books or toys. We are all familiar with parents who send their child to their room as a time-out. The room has all of their playthings, a TV set, a computer, etc. The child can entertain himself in that area for hours and might prefer to be there rather than in another part of the house. Within the school setting, the student should not have access to books, writing utensils or toys. This is not a time to do school work. This is a short period of time, not to exceed five minutes, for the student to regain control.

7. A time-out area is not a busy hallway where many people are passing by and probably are going to talk to the child. This may be more reinforcing to the child than the time spent in the classroom.

8. A time-out area is not sending the child to the office, where there is activity and people are coming in and out. The child may prefer to be there rather than in the classroom.

9. Avoid all talk with the student while he or she is in time-out.

10. Make sure that all staff supervising the use of time-out have been well trained in its appropriate use.

11. For students with autism, time-out may not be appropriate. They may use the time to self-stimulate.

12. If a student is frequently given time-out, use the IEP process to reevaluate its appropriate use.

A better understanding of the use of time-out will result in its effectiveness as an appropriate behavioral intervention. This section has given you helpful guidance on its use. Use this information as you develop policies and procedures and train staff in your district and school building.

References

Johns, B. and Carr, V. (2002). *Techniques for managing verbally and physically aggressive students.* Second Edition. Denver: Love Publishing.

Johns, B. (2002). "The appropriateness of time-out." In Montague, M. and Warger, C. (Editors) (2002), "Afterschool extensions: including students with disabilities in afterschool programs." Reston, VA: *Exceptional Innovations,* 114-116.

Johns, B. et al. (1996). *Best practices for managing adolescents with emotional/behavioral disorders within the school environment.* Reston, VA: Council for Children with Behavioral Disorders.

Lake, S. (2003). "Year to date: top behavior-related cases of 2003." *Special Ed Connection*™.

Norlin, J. (2004). *The Special Education 2004 Desk Book.* Horsham, PA: LRP Publications.

SmartStart: Time-Out. *Special Ed Connection*™. Horsham, PA: LRP Publications.

Sulzer, B. and Mayer, G. (1972). *Behavior modification procedures for school personnel.* Hinsdale, Illinois: The Dryden Press.

Intervention #2 - Positive Reinforcement

Scenarios

To increase the likelihood of student success, school personnel need to increase their use of positive reinforcement throughout the school day. Picture these scenes.

Accentuating the Positive

Mrs. Johnson has a rule in her fourth-grade classroom that students must raise their hands when they have a question to ask her during independent math work. Melissa raises her hand, and Mrs. Johnson, who has been moving around the classroom, sees Melissa and goes over to her and says: "Melissa, thank you for raising your hand. How can I help you?" In the same classroom, Mrs. Johnson has established a system for Mark, another student, who does not like to do math but does like to draw. She has provided him with a sketchpad for his drawing and allows him to draw for two minutes when he has worked on his math for at least five minutes. After assisting Melissa, she looks over at Mark and notices that he has been working on his math for well over five minutes. She walks over to Mark, looks at the math paper, smiles at Mark, and says: " Wow, Mark, you have done 10 problems and they are all correct — way to go. You can take a few minutes and draw in your sketchpad."

Mr. Meeks, a high school teacher, is assigned to hall duty in the morning. Jesse is going down the hall and unknowingly drops a piece of paper out of his notebook. While other students just ignore the event and walk by, Brad observes the action, picks up the piece of paper, and walks up to Jesse to return the paper. Mr. Meeks goes up to Brad and comments: "Brad, I saw the way you picked up that paper and returned it to Jesse. I appreciate what you did — that was kind of you." Mr. Meeks then sees Amanda walking quietly down the hall. He goes up to Amanda and says, "Amanda, thanks for walking quietly in the hall — have a great day."

Mrs. Johnson and Mr. Meeks know the importance of positive reinforcement — they accentuate the positive. They both make frequent positive statements to students — Mrs. Johnson has few behavioral problems in her class, and Mr. Meeks has found that his praise state-ments have reduced hallway problems.

Now, let's look at two other school settings:

Confusing the Positive

Mrs. Smith teaches second grade in the same building as does Mrs. Johnson. During independent work, she notices that Margo is work-ing on her assignment. She looks over at Margo and unenthusiasti-cally says, "Good girl."

Mr. Peterson teaches high school biology. Most of the students in the lab are working on a project, but a few students are not doing what they are supposed to be doing. Mr. Peterson comments: "Great job, class. Keep up the good work."

Mrs. Smith and Mr. Peterson want to recognize appropriate behavior but are "missing the mark." Margo is not sure what she has done to receive the praise — "good girl." Is it because she is staying in her seat or because she is working on the assignment, even though she really has only done one math problem? The students who are on task in Mr. Peterson's biology class hear the reinforcement but recognize that some of their peers aren't working, so they feel it is unfair that all students were praised. On the other hand, the students who are not working recognize that they can "loaf" and still receive praise if some of the students are working. These two teachers need to learn how to appropriately use positive reinforcement.

Definition of Positive Reinforcement

Positive reinforcement is the sincere recognition of an individual by praising, giving a tangible item or allowing a favored activity for appropriate behavior for the purpose of proactively changing inappro-priate behavior within the specific environment, with a resulting increase in appropriate behavior. Reinforcement provides feedback to the student about his/her acceptable behavior. Martin and Pear (2003) define the principle of positive reinforcement as ". . . if, in a given sit-uation, somebody does something that is followed immediately by a positive reinforcer, then that person is more likely to do the same thing again when he or she next encounters a similar situation." (p. 29). Strain and Joseph (2004) assert that it is the primary means by which children learn to take pride in pro-social behavior and that praise increases the likelihood that the pro-social behavior will continue and increase in the future. Positive reinforcement celebrates the accomplishments of an individual.

Positive reinforcement occurs daily in our lives. If a child does something that pleases his/her parent, the parent smiles and/or gives a hug. The child continues to engage in the behavior. An adult does a good job in the workplace and is praised by the supervisor (Sulzer-Azaroff 1977).

Gartin and Murdick (2001) state that the "consequence culture of public schools emphasizes the use of punishment" (p. 348). Research has shown that reactive discipline systems result in increases in problem behaviors rather than improvements (Tidwell, Flannery and Lewis-Palmer 2003). The Individuals with Disabilities Education Act of 2004 makes a strong statement for the need for positive behavioral interventions to see long-term change in student behavior and to move away from this consequence culture of schools. Schools often are referred to as "reinforcement deserts," where students receive few positive statements about their appropriate behaviors. We must turn the tide and assure that our schools are places where students are recognized for "doing the right things." It is critical that school personnel work to increase their use of positive reinforcement. This section outlines how to do just that.

Commonly used types of positive reinforcers can include:

- Primary reinforcers

- Tangible reinforcers

- Social reinforcers

- Token reinforcers

- The Premack Principle

Primary reinforcers can be defined as those that have the effect of maintaining or perpetuating life. In schools, the most common of those would be food. These have been used when teaching specific language or social skills to children with significant behavioral issues. I've used small bites of food as a reinforcer for students with autism in order for them to emit a specific sound. Many people remember the days when staff may have used M&Ms for children as reinforcers. Small pieces of food prevent the child from becoming satiated and the food from becoming ineffective. When primary reinforcers are used, it is critical to know what specific foods the student desires. Also consider the student's health.

As an example, I worked with a student who engaged in very self-injurious behaviors. I was not in favor of using any aversives to eliminate the behavior; yet the student's only reinforcer was bacon. Obviously, bacon could be used only in very small amounts, and such a reinforcer needs to be faded away as quickly as possible. When the student was engaged in productive and interactive behavior, I reinforced him with very small pieces of bacon, but I also paired the bacon with a positive statement. I was able to quickly fade the use of bacon by giving it to the student every time he was engaged in appropriate behavior, then every other time (but still using positive verbal reinforcement), then every third time, again continuing to use verbal positive reinforcement each time. Eventually, I was able to completely eliminate the use of the primary reinforcement and provide only praise for the student. There was no need to use an aversive with the use of appropriate reinforcers.

Schools may use primary reinforcers when they require students to earn a snack contingent on work completion, or they have drawings for soft drinks or provide candy as a reinforcer. School personnel may also have parties with food for students who have engaged in appropriate behavior for a specific period of time.

Tangible reinforcers are items such as trinkets, toys or school supplies. It is always preferred to use small, inexpensive objects, otherwise it becomes very expensive for school personnel, and the student may quickly tire of the items.

Social reinforcers are the most commonly used in the school setting. They include conditioned reinforcers such as attention and verbal statements. The most effective verbal statement is what I refer to as "behavior-specific praise." Rather than the teacher telling the kindergarten student, "Good girl," the teacher praises the specific behavior by describing it: "Maggie, I really like the way you are working quietly at your desk."

Some individuals can reinforce themselves for a good job via intrinsic motivation. However, all of us need praise as a form of feedback to know whether we are doing something that meets with another's approval. Witzel and Mercer (2003) stress that the use of praise may help students with learning disabilities develop an intrinsic purpose for a behavior, and it also will help them in the short term while they have difficulty developing internal control. Reinforcement in the form of praise has been shown to enhance individuals' self-esteem and their use of self-reinforcing statements.

Token reinforcement is a system where the student earns an object that can be exchanged at a later time for another reinforcing activity. Token systems were originally used in psychiatric hospitals. Individuals performed certain tasks and received tokens, which they could then exchange at a designated time for items or privileges. Tokens are given immediately following the emission of a correct response, and then a specific number of those tokens are designated to earn the back-up reinforcer. In a classroom, students may earn stars, and a given number of stars earn the student a privilege. Some schools give students stars for each book report they complete, and then offer a prize for a given number of stars — this is a token system. Point systems would be classified as token reinforcers. (An entire section of this book will be devoted to point systems.)

Lastly, Premack (1959) gave us another positive reinforcer that became known as the **Premack Principle**. High-frequency behaviors the student desires can be used to reinforce low-frequency behaviors the student desires less. Here's an example: A student loves to draw pictures (desired, high-frequency behavior), but he does not want to do a math worksheet (undesirable, low-frequency behavior). The teacher might determine that if the student works five minutes on the math worksheet or completes five math problems successfully, the student can draw a picture for two minutes. In order for the educator to use the Premack Principle, he must observe the student for a period of time to determine which activities are high-frequency, desirable activities and which are low-frequency, undesirable ones. Another method is to interview the parent and the student to determine preferable activities.

In the behavior analysis literature there are eight basic schedules for providing reinforcement. Ratio schedules, either variable or fixed, make reinforcement contingent on the child emitting a certain number of responses. Simple interval schedules, either fixed or variable, make reinforcement dependent on a response being made after a certain time period has elapsed. Duration schedules make reinforcement dependent on a response being made for a certain continuous period of time.

A common form of an interval schedule reinforcer is the popular "timer game" designed to gain appropriate behavior from students. The teacher sets the timer at a fixed interval of every five minutes or at variable intervals. When the timer goes off, students who are in their seats and working productively receive some type of reinforcer.

Correct Use of Positive Reinforcement

As discussed earlier, positive reinforcement should be provided sincerely and immediately after the emission of appropriate behavior. B.F. Skinner (1938) taught us that immediate reinforcement is more effective than delayed reinforcement. In the scenarios above, Mrs. Johnson and Mr. Meeks engaged in immediate reinforcement of the students who were engaging in appropriate behaviors.

General praise vs. behavior specific praise

Although it is better than saying nothing, general praise such as "good girl" or "nice job" is not as effective as behavior-specific praise. You can teach the child what the desirable behavior is when you are specific. For instance, if Jenny is sitting in her seat and working, and the teacher approaches Jenny and says, "Good girl," Jenny is wondering what she is doing that makes her a good girl. She may believe she is a good girl because she stays in her seat. A more preferable method is to describe the desired behavior in the praise statement: "Jenny, I really appreciated the way you raised your hand when you had a question." Other examples of behavior specific praise include:

"Cindy, I really appreciated the way you shared the toy with Bill."

"Jay, thanks for walking quietly in the hall."

"Bill, you really worked hard on that test."

Assuring the use of positive reinforcement

Educators must always monitor their use of reinforcement. For every corrective statement made to a student, there should be four positive statements made. When teachers see an increase in behavior problems in their classrooms, it is critical that they examine their own behavior. Are they reprimanding for negative behavior while infrequently using positive statements? Here are some practical ways educators can monitor their use of positive reinforcement:

1. Audiotape a period of time within the classroom. The teacher can record a 30- to 60-minute period, listen to the tape at the end of the day and make a tally of the number of praise statements per student. The teacher can then set a goal for increasing those positive statements. Each week, the teacher can tape a segment of time to see whether the use of praise statements is increasing.

2. Make a tally of the number of praise statements made during a specific period of time and chart that use at intervals over several weeks.

3. Use pennies to count positive statements. The teacher puts a number of pennies in one pocket. Each time the teacher makes a sincere praise statement, she moves a penny from one pocket to another with the goal of moving all the pennies from one pocket to the other pocket relatively quickly.

4. Play a game with the students. Fill up the jar with "praise pennies." Each time the teacher notes appropriate behavior

from one of the students, she puts a penny in the jar. When the jar is full, the students receive a special treat.

5. Work with a paraprofessional to monitor each other's use of praise statements. Keep a tally of the other's use of praise and discuss the results at the end of the day.

6. Praise stickers. For younger students, the teacher can tape charts to the students' desks, purchase smiley face stickers, and, when students are engaging in appropriate behavior, he can verbally reinforce the specific behavior and give the student a sticker for the chart. The teacher should set a goal for how many he'll give out each day. For older students, the teacher may want to make small labels (size of address labels) with praise statements such as, "Thanks for raising your hand," "Thanks for working quietly," "You did an awesome job of paying attention today," etc. When a student is working, the teacher can go over to the student and put one of the labels on the student's work or on a notebook.

7. Praise bingo. I was teaching a class for general education teachers on positive strategies, when one of the teachers came up with this idea to increase her use of positive reinforcement and to subsequently improve the behavior of her students. She made bingo cards for each student. In each square of the bingo card, she put praise statements that she might make to students. When she made a praise statement and it was on a student's bingo card, the student got to color in the square of the bingo card. For an example of this, see Johns, B. (2002). *The Paraprofessional's Guide to Managing Student Behavior* (video workbook), LRP Publications.

Reducing primary, tangible or token reinforcement over time: The Premack Principle

The ultimate goal for our students is to teach them how to be intrinsically motivated. In order to do this, we must teach them how to recognize their own appropriate behavior and reward themselves. We must teach them to make positive statements about self and others. To achieve that goal, we must reduce primary, tangible or token reinforcement as quickly as possible. This can be done using a fading procedure. Always pair the use of primary or tangible reinforcers with praise. Begin a program by rewarding a student every time he emits an appropriate response, then begin fading out the tangible item by rewarding every other time, then every third time and so on. However, continue to use praise with the student and teach the child how to make positive comments to himself. With the Premack Principle, the object is to lengthen the amount of time the student can stay on a task he desires less without earning the desired activity. Example: Start with the student working on a task for five minutes and then receiving two minutes on the desired activity.

Dealing with students who misbehave after receiving positive reinforcement

The adult should continue to reinforce, even when the student becomes negative immediately after the praise is delivered. There is a phenomenon that occurs with some students that I've seen many times in my career. The adult makes a positive statement to a student, and the student begins acting out. The natural reaction of the adult is to quit reinforcing the student because of fear that the praise will result in negative behavior. Don't let this happen. The adult should continue to reinforce the child and teach the child how to accept the reinforcement. Accepting a compliment is a social skill that must be taught. The child may be testing the adult to see if the adult is just, as he has experienced, like everyone else has been — making negative statements to the child. Children with behavioral problems are "reprimand magnets" and may set themselves up for negative statements. Hang in there with them and stress what they do right.

A teacher I knew used a "compliment cup" in her classroom of primary-age students with behavioral disorders. She taught her children examples of how to give sincere compliments and how to accept a compliment. Each day, students would come into the classroom and draw the name of another student. The students were responsible for giving at least three sincere compliments to the students whose names they drew that day. When the teacher heard the compliment statement, she would praise the student for making the statement. Those students' behaviors were excellent because of the number of praise statements used in the classroom. The students also would compliment others outside their classroom.

Public vs. private praise statements

Educators must know the student to determine whether praise should be delivered publicly or privately. Some students, particularly younger students, love to be praised in front of other students. In the process of giving praise to one student, the others might also start engaging in the same behavior so they too can receive praise. Other students prefer to be reinforced privately, to avoid embarrassment in front of their peers. Remember that other reinforcers are present in the classroom. Bill may make faces at Roberta in the classroom and gain more recognition from Roberta than he receives from a teacher who praises him when he is on task. Bill also wants to avoid ridicule from his peers for his conformity to the school rules. The classroom environment and the needs of the individual student must be assessed when determining whether to praise publicly or in private.

Fairness

Many adults are hesitant to use positive reinforcement, especially when it involves primary or tangible reinforcers, because they believe it is not fair to the other students in the class. Certainly this argument is not valid regarding praise, since the educator should frequently provide positive praise to all students who are complying with the educator's expectations. However, when there is a need to increase behavior of a particular student, Sulzer-Azaroff and Mayer (1977) offer this response in their classic behavior analysis textbook: "It is standard for teachers to provide students with different learning materials reflecting their current levels of functioning. Similarly, appropriate reinforcers must be provided for academic and social behaviors if learning is to occur." (p. 114). They also point to research showing that, more often than not, once a special reinforcement program has been designed for a single student, the whole group improves. Fellow students appear relieved at times and may even cheer the success of the student who has previously had problems.

Cautions in the Use of Positive Reinforcements

1. One of the most common mistakes made in schools is unintentionally providing positive reinforcement for inappropriate behavior, resulting in an increase in that inappropriate behavior. I remember a teacher who was very frustrated in her

work with a student we will call Nancy. The teacher could not figure out why Nancy's negative behavior was increasing. The teacher decided to videotape her classroom. When she viewed the video, she immediately saw what was wrong. When Nancy was quiet and on-task, the teacher was leaving her alone. When Nancy started making inappropriate noises and throwing papers, the teacher would go over and pay attention to Nancy. Thus, the teacher reinforced the inappropriate behavior.

2. When school personnel are using primary reinforcers or a token reinforcement system, it is critical that they always pair reinforcement delivery with a verbal behavior-specific praise statement. Then the primary reinforcer or the token reinforcement can be faded away and the adult can continue using the praise statements.

3. School personnel must assure that their use of praise is sincere, that they mean what they say to the student. At times adults may become mechanical in their use of praise, and the student knows that it is not sincere. The praise then is not reinforcing to the student.

4. Avoid the common "you did well, but . . ." statement. There are times when an adult will make a positive statement praising the student for a task performed when asked, but then the adult adds what I call a zinger: ". . . but you should have done it the first time I asked you." Such statements are not reinforcing to the student because they end up being negative in the student's view.

5. Questions continually arise about group vs. individual reinforcement contingencies. Educators must be very careful about the use of group contingencies. They can be very effective for some students. As an example, a principal I knew was concerned about cafeteria behavior in her K-6 building, so she made some large, blank laminated bingo cards — one for each classroom — and put them on the wall. The rules for cafeteria behavior were posted in the room and reviewed periodically. When an entire class followed the rules for that

lunch period, she colored in a square of the bingo card. When the class had a bingo, she brought in a dessert or a big cookie for the class. The system worked and improved cafeteria behavior and the students encouraged each other to follow the rules. Generally, such systems are effective. However, they must be monitored very closely. There may have been a student in one of the classes who preferred to misbehave so the whole group would not get the prize. Or there may be a student who is having particular difficulty on a given day and prevents the class from getting a bingo square filled in and the other students might retaliate against him.

We must all work to increase our use of positive reinforcement throughout our schools. By doing so effectively and sincerely, we will improve the behavior of our students.

References

Gartin, B. and Murdick, N. (2001). A new IDEA mandate: the use of functional assessment of behavior and positive behavior supports. *Remedial and Special Education*, 22(6), 344-349.

Johns, B. (2002). *The Paraprofessional's Guide to Managing Student Behavior* (video workbook). Horsham, PA: LRP Publications.

Martin, G. and Pear, J. (2003). *Behavior modification: what it is and how to do it*. Upper Saddle River, New Jersey: Prentice-Hall.

Premack, D. (1959). Toward empirical behavior laws: 1. positive reinforcement. *Psychological Review*, 66, 219-233.

Skinner, B. F. (1938). *The behavior of organisms*. New York: Appleton-Century-Crofts.

Strain, P. and Joseph, G. (2004). A not so good job with "good job." *Journal of Positive Behavioral Interventions*, 6(1), 55-59.

Sulzer-Azaroff, B. and Mayer, G. (1977). *Applying behavior-analysis procedures with children and youth*. New York: Holt, Rinehart, and Winston.

Tidwell, A., Flannery, K., and Lewis-Palmer, T. (2003). A description of elementary classroom discipline referral patterns. *Preventing School Failure*, 48(1), 18-26.

Witzel, B. and Mercer, C. (2003). Using rewards to teach students with disabilities: Implications for motivation. *Remedial and Special Education*. 24(2), 88-96.

Intervention #3 – Physical Intervention

Within recent years, deaths have occurred within schools when students were restrained inappropriately. Such incidents have caused all school personnel to reflect and rethink the use of physical intervention. A case that generated public dismay was reported in the *Kalamazoo Gazette* in 2003. A student with autism died on the first day of school after being physically restrained by several school staff members after the student experienced seizure-type symptoms and became agitated. When the parent arrived at the school, she found her son face down on the floor being restrained by at least four adults.

Very strict criteria should be established for the use of restraint. Physical intervention in schools should never be used except as a very last resort, when all other interventions have failed and when the student is harming himself or others. Because of the possibility of serious injury during the practice of restraint, an increasing number of states have developed laws and regulations to govern such practices. Policies and procedures also must stress the importance of positive interventions for the student's appropriate behavior.

Let's look at these situations.

Scenarios

Appropriate Use of Physical Intervention – Scenario #1

Josh, a fifth-grader, starts yelling and screaming in the classroom and then begins banging his head on his desk. Mrs. Riley approaches Josh and states very calmly and quietly: "Josh, I need you to stop that. I can't let you hurt yourself. If you continue, I will have to call for the team to take you to time-out." Josh bangs his head again. Again in a calm voice, the teacher calls over the intercom for assistance to her classroom using a pre-designated code for the team to come. The trained team of four individuals arrives within a minute and sees Josh banging his head. The team leader quietly directs the team to use an escort to get Josh out of his desk and out of the classroom. The team uses latex gloves in the restraint. When the team gets Josh to the time-out room, he has calmed down. The team leader directs the staff to release Josh and step away. The team leader praises Josh for calming himself and moves away from him, giving him a few minutes to further calm down.

Appropriate Use of Physical Intervention – Scenario #2

Jill is a kindergarten student in Mr. Alberts' class. The class is out at recess, and, while the class is engaged in a game, Jill becomes angry because she is not winning and begins to bite one of her classmates. Mr. Alberts tells Jill to stop that right away and calls for assistance from the trained team. The team comes to escort Jill off the playground to time-out. Jill is screaming all the way and trying to bite the team members. The team leader directs the other team members to utilize a restraint for which they have been trained and believe is appropriate for Jill. They do not use a floor restraint. The team leader states quietly that when Jill is quiet, the team members will begin to release her. When Jill is quiet for a minute, team members release her and have her stand quietly for a few minutes until they are sure she is ready to leave time-out. The team leader has determined that she will take Jill back to the classroom and stay with her, rather than letting her return to the playground.

In each of these cases, the team leader documented the incidents in writing by providing the following information: name of student, time of restraint, how long the restraint lasted, type of restraint used, individuals involved in the restraint, and incidents leading up to the restraint. The team leader then signed and dated the forms and gave it to the administrator, who sent a copy home to the parent and kept a copy of the incident report in the student's temporary record.

The administrator, teachers, and the team leader discussed the incident at the end of the school day. They discussed what could be done to prevent the incidents from happening again — Are the students receiving enough positive reinforcement when they are behaving appropriately? Is Josh being given positive attention when he is on task? Is Jill being given positive attention when she is playing with other students appropriately on the playground?

The administrator called the parents of both students as soon as possible. The administrator also called the parent of the student who was bitten. And the school nurse was called to assess the severity of the bite so the school could quickly provide that information to the student's parents and determine appropriate medical measures.

In both of these examples of the correct use of physical intervention, the students were physically harming self or others. Obviously, school personnel cannot allow a student to harm him/herself. The teachers did attempt to calm the students and also warned each student about what would happen.

In Jill's case, Mr. Alberts also requested Jill to stop and called the team. He feared that Jill might bite the same student again or bite another student, and he did not want to take that risk. Neither of these students was in special education. If they had been, it would have been critical to include the use of physical intervention in the behavioral intervention plan (BIP) of the individualized education program (IEP) for these students. This intervention is very restrictive.

In Josh's case, the team should be considering a case study evaluation, including a functional behavioral assessment, to gain more information about Josh's specific needs.

Now let's look at incidents where physical intervention is used inappropriately.

Inappropriate Use of Physical Intervention – Scenario #1

Alex is a high school student in Mr.Werner's English class. Alex likes to consider himself the class clown and is "putting on a show" in class. Mr. Werner has had a long day and is tired of Alex's "shenanigans." Mr. Werner says loudly in the classroom, already made noisy by Alex's escapades, "That's it, Alex, go to the office." Alex responds: "You can't make me." Mr. Werner is not happy with that comment and goes over to Alex and says, "Yes, I can make you."

Thinking to himself that he is going to show Mr. Werner who is in charge of the class (and it isn't Mr. Werner), Alex responds, "You can't make me, you're not man enough to make me." This makes Mr. Werner even angrier, and he says to Alex, "Yes, I can make you." He then takes Alex by the arm and proceeds to try to get him out of the classroom.

Alex, of course, does not go willingly and struggles physically with Mr. Werner. They finally end up in the hall and someone else comes along and assists Mr. Werner. When Alex gets home that evening, he has marks on his body as a result of the struggle. Alex reports this to his parents. His parents become angry and start calling other parents whose children also have witnessed the event and report that Mr. Werner did physically intervene with Alex. Alex's parents pick up the phone and report Mr. Werner to the police for physically hurting their child.

Inappropriate Use of Physical Intervention – Scenario #2

Jimmy is a kindergarten student in Mrs. Leeks' class. Jimmy refuses to stay in his seat, and Mrs. Leeks decides she is going to tie him in his chair. Jimmy is left tied to his chair in the classroom for onehour. When Jimmy's mother finds out about this intervention, she is incensed and goes immediately to the building principal who knew nothing about Mrs. Leeks' action.

There are multiple problems with the actions of Mr. Werner and Mrs. Leeks. Both individuals took unilateral action and used physical intervention inappropriately. One may argue that Alex's and Jimmy's actions were inappropriate, but the behaviors did not necessitate the actions the teachers took. What could Mr. Werner and Mrs. Leeks have done to prevent these unfortunate events from happening? Alex was being inappropriate in his class, and Mr. Werner could not teach as a result.

Mr. Werner could have moved over to the area where Alex was and reminded him of the classroom rules. If Alex continued, he could have stated quietly to Alex, "Alex, I need you to begin your work." If Alex started his work, he could have thanked him. If Alex continued to disrupt, Mr. Werner could have stated quietly, "Alex, I need you to start your work. If you continue to disrupt the class, I will need you to go to the office."

If Alex yells out again, Mr. Werner could state: "Alex, I need you to go to the office. You can either walk on your own or I will get assistance to escort you. It's your choice." If Alex calms down, Mr. Werner would thank him. If Alex does not, Mr. Werner would go to the intercom and call for assistance.

Staff should never get into a confrontation with a student in front of the class, particularly at the middle and high school ages. Students want to save face in front of their peers and are going to show staff who is in charge of the class. Likewise, staff should never get into a one-on-one physical confrontation with a student. This is a lawsuit waiting to happen.

In the case of Jimmy and Mrs. Leeks, the teacher should have sought assistance from the administrator and other personnel within the school. She should have looked for positive interventions for Jimmy when he was sitting in his seat.

Definition of Physical Intervention

The two most common forms of restraint used within public schools are "manual restraints" and "mechanical restraints."

"Manual restraint" refers to the restriction of a student's freedom of movement or physical activity by adult(s) using their own bodies to restrict that movement. It is also referred to as "therapeutic holding." The purpose of such restraint is to allow the student to regain self-control or to maintain safety for other students within the environment.

"Mechanical restraint" involves the use of a device such as a blanket or a tie-down as a method of restricting a student's freedom of movement or physical activity.

The origins of restraint date back to early psychiatric hospitals. Ryan and Peterson (2004) report the use of physical restraint being applied to children with emotional disturbances since the 1950s. Now with the inclusion of students with significant emotional/behavioral disorders within the public schools, there is an increase in its use. As a result, more states are establishing specific laws and regulations to govern its use. Whether your state has specific laws and regulations or not, school districts should establish their own policies and procedures for using restraints. School district personnel also must follow state-specific laws and regulations.

Punishment vs. preventing harm

Physical intervention should not be conducted as punishment; rather, it should be used as a means to assist the student in regaining self-control or in preventing a student from harming self or others. In an 8th U.S. Circuit Court of Appeals case — *Golden v. Anders, et al.,* 02-2702 (March 28, 2003) — the court ruled in favor of the school district because the principal was attempting to diffuse a volatile situ-

31

ation and was not punishing the student. The case involved a principal restraining an elementary school student after the student violently kicked a vending machine and resisted efforts to settle down. In this case, the teacher had attempted to quiet down the student but was unsuccessful, and the student's escalating behavior created a need for the principal to restrain him. (*School Law Briefings*, July 2003, LRP Publications.)

Another 8th Circuit decision, *Heidemann v. Rother*, 24 IDELR 167 (8th Cir. 1996), involved the use of a mechanical restraint in the form of "blanket wrapping." The child was a 9-year-old with significant disabilities. The courts ruled that the blanket wrapping — "binding the body with a blanket so the child could not use her arms, legs, or hands" (Norlin and Raphael 2003, p. 10) — did not violate the female student's constitutional rights to due process and was not an unreasonable restraint. According to Norlin and Raphael (2003), the court stressed the importance of utilizing the standard of *Youngberg v. Romeo*, 457 U.S. 307 (1982). That case concerned the restraint of an adult with mental retardation in a state-operated hospital where he was involuntarily committed. The *Youngberg* standard "is whether a district's use of an aversive technique involving physical restraint constituted a substantial departure from accepted professional judgment, practice or standards. Only when there is such a departure are constitutional rights implicated." (Norlin and Raphael 2003, p. 11).

In another case, *CJN by SKN v. Minneapolis Public Schools*, 38 IDELR 208 (8th Cir. 2003), a third-grader with significant emotional disturbance was restrained. The majority of the restraints lasted less than a minute, but on several occasions, when the student began kicking others, hitting staff or banging his head, he was restrained for five or more minutes. The court upheld the use of restraint in this case because the district made a good faith effort to assist the child in achieving his goals. The court stated it regretted that the student was subjected to the restraints, but that did not make his education an inappropriate one.

Ryan and Peterson (2004) conducted an extensive search and were unable to identify any research indicating how widespread the use of physical restraint is within the public schools. Restraint also has not been researched as an educational intervention. The Children's Health Act of 2000 did establish standards regarding the use of physical restraint in psychiatric facilities, but they do not apply to schools.

Correct Use of Physical Intervention

Prior to using physical restraint of any kind, school districts must establish policies and procedures for its use. Such policies should include these critical components:

1. References to specific state laws and regulations that apply.

2. Definition of physical restraint.

3. When physical restraint is appropriate.

4. Parental notice requirements.

5. The importance of the use of positive behavioral interventions for the student when he/she engages in appropriate behavior.

6. The types of restraints that are acceptable within the school system.

7. Procedures for documentation.

For students in special education programs, the use of physical intervention must be included as a restrictive intervention within the student's IEP. Intervention plans also should be included in the Section 504 plans for students who are eligible for services under Section 504 of the Rehabilitation Act. Physical intervention must be only one part of an intervention plan that also should include positive interventions and less restrictive interventions. If repeated incidents precipitating the need for physical intervention occur, then the IEP team must reconvene to determine the appropriateness of the intervention.

Watch for medical contraindications

Any medical contraindications must be considered within the scope of the plan. Certain restraints may be inappropriate for students because of their medical problems. Even for students who have no apparent medical contraindications, it is critical that, during any restraint, staff watch for signs of medical distress, such as difficulty breathing. Ryan and Peterson (2004) recommend that staff utilizing physical restraint also receive certification in first aid and CPR (car-

33

diopulmonary resuscitation) in the event of an emergency during the restraint.

Staff training should focus on preventing harm

School personnel must always remember that restraint should only be used when the student is endangering self or others. In two federal Office for Civil Rights rulings, teachers taped the mouths of students for excessive talking. (*Oakland (CA) Unified Sch. Dist.*, 20 IDELR 1338 (OCR 1993) and *Aiken County (SC) Sch. Dist.*, 23 IDELR 113 (OCR 1995).) Such actions on the part of school personnel were inappropriate, OCR found. While talking out might be unsatisfactory to a teacher, it by no means warrants restraint.

All staff using physical restraint should receive adequate and ongoing training to minimize the risk of injury to the student. According to Caruso (2002), proper training is critical, both from a practical and a legal standpoint. All staff should first be trained in the appropriate use of positive interventions for students and de-escalation strategies for aggressive behavior. Staff chosen to be on the physical restraint team should be individuals who are good at handling a crisis, are able to remain calm and professional, and are consistent in their techniques.

The team approach works best

A team approach should be used. I do not recommend any type of restraint by one individual unless it is an emergency situation. When more than one individual conducts the restraint, each person can check the behavior and pressure the others are using. More than one individual also means witnesses in the event a staff member is accused of inappropriate behavior. (Remember our earlier examples of inappropriate physical intervention, where staff acted unilaterally and created problem situations.)

A group of four to five people should constitute a well-trained team thoroughly versed in the use of physical restraint. It is important to balance the use of as many people as necessary to ensure safety with the need to avoid placing undue pressure on the student. Team restraint also sends a message to students: "We work as a team. This is not a personal challenge." When establishing a team of individuals, school personnel should also establish a plan for covering team members' classrooms when they are called to an emergency.

All precautions should be taken to ensure the safety of the student, and those precautions should be considered on the IEP if the student is in special education. For instance, a helmet may need to be used when restraining a student who is head banging. All staff involved in the restraint should use latex gloves.

Team leader responsibilities

It is important to designate a team leader who is responsible for any verbal instructions given. Team members should not engage in conversation with a student during a restraint. The team leader lets the student know that the team will release the student when he or she becomes calm.

It is also important that the team leader remove items from the student that may cause harm to the student or to the staff involved in the restraint. As an example, the student may have a pencil or pen that he may poke at himself or at staff. The team leader should let the student know that the object will be removed and that it will be returned when the student is calm. If a student is prone to physical aggression, staff will want to talk with parents about the need for their cooperation in assuring that the student does not wear items such as cowboy boots that hurt when the student kicks at the staff. For a student with special needs, this should be delineated on his/her IEP behavioral intervention plan. If, however, the student is in restraint and is wearing boots, it is advisable for the staff to remove the boots and return them when the student is calm.

Choosing restraint methods and training programs

Floor restraint should be used only as a last resort. This is by far the most restrictive restraint and one that can result in more injuries than others.

There are a number of physical intervention training programs for school district personnel. When choosing a particular method of restraint and employing individuals to conduct the training, it is important to check specific information about the restraint method. Following are some questions you will want to ask:

1. How long have the individuals or company been training in the use of physical restraint? What actual school experience do the trainers have?

2. What is the history of injuries from their specific type of restraint?

3. Do they have references of other school district personnel that they have trained?

4. What is the specific curriculum of the training? Does the training also provide positive interventions and verbal de-escalation strategies?

5. What type of follow-up services are provided?

6. How often is training provided to the staff?

7. What is the cost of the training?

8. Will those being trained have the opportunity for practice, and how will their skills be measured?

9. Are appropriate self-defense strategies included?

It is also important that all staff be trained in methods of self-defense. In some cases, a student may try to bite or choke a staff member. Staff members should know how to handle such an incident to protect themselves until assistance arrives.

Document everything

Any incident of physical restraint must be documented in writing. Documentation forms should include the following information:

1. Name of student.

2. Date and time of incident.

3. Events leading up to the restraint.

4. Other interventions utilized.

5. Length of time the student was restrained.

6. Names of staff members involved.

7. Type of restraint used.

8. Behavior during and after the restraint.

9. The form should be signed and dated and include the position of the person completing the form.

The incident form should be kept in the student's temporary record and wherever else district policy requires. A copy of the incident report should be sent to the parent/guardian.

Cautions in the Use of Physical Intervention

1. Be sure to review any state laws or rules and regulations that govern the administration of physical intervention within the schools. Some states have established very specific laws, rules and regulations concerning the use of physical intervention.

2. Before anyone engages in physical intervention of a student, he or she must be thoroughly trained. When providing training for staff to use physical intervention, always include the use of positive interventions to improve behavior and preventive techniques designed to de-escalate a crisis. I received many calls from schools that only wanted physical intervention training. I consistently refused to do that, because it is critical that staff members know how to positively recognize appropriate behavior, deal with children's frustrations, and de-escalate a crisis.

3. Monitor all use of physical restraint. At the end of the school day, debrief team members involved in any restraint that has been employed. Discuss whether it was appropriate or could have been done differently. If restraint is being used frequently with a particular student, it is a clue to staff that it may not be effective for that particular student, and that other more appropriate interventions should be examined.

4. Avoid putting off writing the incident report. Do so as soon as possible after the incident occurs. In reality, the longer school personnel wait to write up an event that has occurred, the more likely they are to forget critical components of the event.

5. Be very cautious of the sex of the individual utilizing the restraint. As an example, it may not be appropriate for a male staff member to restrain a high school girl who may receive some sexual gratification from the restraint. Likewise, it may

not be appropriate for a female staff member to restrain a high school male. We do recognize that there may be times when such a restraint needs to occur; in those instances, the staff members must be very cognizant of where their body parts are touching the student.

6. An individual who is angry with a student should not be involved in the restraint. It is possible that the individual might unconsciously put undue pressure on the student — not engaging in "therapeutic holding."

7. Restraint that prevents a student from breathing or speaking should not be used.

8. Whenever possible give the student a warning that if he or she harms someone or self, he or she will be restrained. But give students every opportunity to control their own behavior.

9. Never restrain a student any longer than is absolutely necessary. Let the student know (via the team leader speaking in a very calm voice) that as soon as the student becomes calm and quiet, you will begin the process of releasing him/her. Praise the student for becoming quiet. When the student is calm, move away from the student for a short period of time (not to exceed five minutes), and then the team leader should discuss the event with the student if the student is capable of processing cognitively. The adult will want to ask the student these questions: Tell me what happened; what did you do; and what could you do the next time this happens. Then prepare the student for return to the classroom environment by talking to the student about what will be expected of him/her after he/she returns to the classroom. Leave the student with a positive statement such as: "I know you can have a good rest of the day."

10. Avoid letting students "bait" any staff member. All staff should work together as a team. Johns and Carr (2002) warn that students may try to bait a staff member into intervening alone. The student might say: "You think you're so big. Why don't you try to make me go to time-out." Response from

staff should be a very calm statement: "In this school, we work together as a team. No one will force someone else to do something."

11. Whenever possible, physical intervention should not be done in front of other students. It is more respectful of the student to try to escort him or her to a private area, such as a time-out room. If the team is unable to get the student to a private area, then it is preferable to clear the room of other students in order to protect them and to provide privacy for the student being restrained.

12. Be very cautious that restraint is not, in fact, reinforcing to the student. Jones and Timber (2002) stress that at the point of the actual restraint, the individual being restrained may have produced a "powerful dose of another well-documented reinforcer; i.e., s/he has captured the undivided attention, albeit negative, of every adult in the vicinity." (p. 39).

Even though physical intervention should be used as a last resort, all schools should be prepared in the event that a student endangers him/herself or others. Preparation requires a review of state laws and regulations, development of school district policies and procedures, training of all staff, and increased use of positive interventions to prevent such incidents.

References

Estes, S. (2003). Death probe frustrates mom. *Kalamazoo Gazette.*

Johns, B. and Carr, V. (2002). *Techniques for managing verbally and physically aggressive students.* (2nd edition). Denver: Love Publishing.

Jones, R. and Timbers, G. (2002). An analysis of the restraint event and its behavioral effects on clients and staff. *Reclaiming children and youth*, 11(1), 37-41.

Lake, S. (Editor) (2003). 8th Cir. Backs principal's restraint of student who attacked vending machine. *School Law Briefings.*7(3), 5.

Norlin, J. and Raphael, F. (2003). *Aversives in the classroom: What are the legal limits?* Horsham, PA: LRP Publications.

Ryan, J. and Peterson, R. (2004). Physical restraint in schools. *Behavioral Disorders*, 29(2), 154-168.

Intervention #4 – Police Intervention

While many large high schools have employed security officers for a number of years, some school officials remain reluctant to call the police when students have committed criminal offenses. Presumably, these school personnel fear they will be viewed as an unsafe school and receive negative publicity in the community. However, major crimes that occurred in Arkansas, Oregon and Colorado schools in the late 1990s brought school safety into a spotlight that could not be ignored. Congress addressed the use of police with special education students when it reauthorized the Individuals with Disabilities Education Act in 1997. The end result: Students who commit criminal activities in the schools should face the legal consequences of their crimes.

Scenarios

Appropriate Use of Police Intervention

Liz and Marie, seventh-graders at Sunnyside School, are in the hall between classes. Staff members are in the hall monitoring. Liz and Marie become agitated and start yelling at each other. Liz threatens to hit Marie. A staff member approaches and speaks calmly to Liz: "Liz, I need you to come with me." Liz yells she is going to slug Marie. The staff member, Mr. Lawrence, says: "We have a rule in this school that if you strike someone, I will have to report it, and the police will be called. Make a good decision for yourself and come with me." Liz then slaps Marie very hard in the face. In the meantime, another staff member has approached. The other staff member requests that Marie come with her to the nurse's office. When Marie is gone, Liz becomes quiet and walks to the office with Mr. Lawrence.

Mr. Lawrence reports the incident and the specific events immediately to the principal, who calls the police. Indeed, a crime has been committed, and an adult witnessed the event. The police arrive on the scene and interview the principal, Mr. Lawrence and the other staff member who witnessed the event. The police officer then interviews Marie and Liz. The principal calls Liz's parents and informs them that Liz has committed a crime and is being taken to the police department. The principal also calls Marie's parents to report what has happened to Marie and to report that she was slapped in the face but does not require additional medical assistance.

Liz is arrested and taken to the police department, where her parents will have to pick her up.

Sunnyside School had established policies and procedures, in cooperation with the local police department, on the use of police intervention in the schools. The policies and procedures also had been adopted by the school board. All parents of students attending the school had received copies of and been trained on the policies and procedures. Remember also that Mr. Lawrence provided a warning to Liz that if she hit Marie, the police would be called and charges would be pressed.

Now let's look at these examples:

Inappropriate Use of Police Intervention – Scenario #1

Principal Kevin Carter is frustrated by the behavior of students who misbehave in the halls. He does hall duty and corrects those students who are running in the hall. He has had to correct Steve every morning for running in the hall. One morning, Steve is running in the hall again and bumps into one of the girls who begins to cry. Mr. Carter is fed up with Steve and says, "That's it, I'm calling the police." He does so, and the police arrive. The police officer is not happy with Mr. Carter. Mr. Carter insists that he wants to press charges against Steve for running in the hall and bumping into the girl. The police tell Mr. Carter that he can legally press charges under a disorderly conduct code. Mr. Carter also says that an additional charge should be made because Steve ran into the girl. The police officer then questions the principal more, questions the girl, and then questions Steve. He determines that Steve did not mean to harm the girl. He therefore informs the principal that he can arrest Steve on a disorderly conduct charge, but he does not prefer to do so. Mr. Carter insists and Steve is arrested.

Inappropriate Use of Police Intervention – Scenario #2

Mrs. Evans logs on to her computer at school when she arrives one morning. She finds an e-mail from one of the students. In the e-mail he says he hates her and threatens to kill her with his gun. Mrs. Evans is very upset and immediately reports the incident to the principal, Mr. Arthur, who says he will take care of this internally. The student is in her fourth-period class that day and appears very angry but does not say anything to her and just sits with his head down on his desk. Mrs. Evans, out of fear, does not confront him. At the end of the day, Mrs. Evans goes to Mr. Arthur to see what he has done about the situation. Mr. Arthur says he has decided not to pursue any further action. He says he confronted the student, and the student said he was only kidding.

In the first incident, Principal Carter could have dealt with hallway problems in ways other than police intervention. He could have increased hall monitors. He could have monitored the hall by establishing positive relationships with students, praising students who are acting appropriately in the hall, and talking privately with Steve about the need to walk in the hall to assure school safety. Technically, Steve's behavior could be considered disorderly conduct, but when school officials enlist the police for such minor behaviors, the police may not be as eager to respond when a major event occurs.

In the second incident, Principal Arthur failed to protect the safety of his teachers. This was an open threat to kill the teacher, and he should have reported it immediately to the police.

Definition of Police Intervention

For purposes of this discussion, police intervention can be defined as contact with local law enforcement when a student has committed a criminal act on school property, while attending a school-sponsored event, or even after leaving school property. It also should be noted that the police could be of great assistance to school personnel in providing educational programs for students and staff. Police officials also can provide significant input into policies and procedures for such areas as use of police intervention, bomb threats, vandalism, etc.

Correct Use of Police Intervention

School districts must establish policies that outline police involvement with the school, and districts must demonstrate that police will be called for students with and without disabilities in the event of certain criminal events. The federal Office for Civil Rights has determined that the policy is equally applicable to students with and without disabilities. (*Chester Upland (PA) Sch. Dist.*, 24 IDELR 79 (OCR 1995).) The student, in this case, was a Section 504-eligible student who got into a fight with another student. OCR found the district's actions in calling the police did not violate the student's behavior management component to his educational placement. The agency found no document expressly precluding district officials from calling the police. OCR has ruled that school officials have a duty to protect the health and safety of students and employees, and OCR will not disturb that responsibility. (SmartStart: Discipline under Section 504, *Special Ed Connection*™, LRP Publications.)

In fact, school personnel have an obligation to protect the health, safety and welfare of students. They must call the police when certain criminal activities take place. To fail to do so would be negligent. School personnel must also be familiar with federal and state laws and regulations governing student or staff actions that must be reported to the police.

If police intervention has been deemed inappropriate for a student with a disability, it should be outlined on the behavioral intervention plan of the student's IEP. At times, there may be students for whom police intervention is not appropriate. For instance, a student with severe mental retardation may not have an understanding that some behaviors are criminal behaviors and may fling his/her arms and hit someone. Likewise, a 4-year-old may spit at another child but does not understand that this is a crime; the child needs to be taught that such behavior is not appropriate. Decisions about the appropriateness of calling the police when a student has significant retardation or is very young should be discussed on an individual basis. Some schools may deem it inappropriate to call the police for students as young as 8 years old; on the other hand, I have known 8-year-olds who already were on probation for criminal activities in the community.

School personnel should document, in writing, any incident involving the police. It is very helpful if the school's reporting form closely resembles the police incident report, which makes it easier to compare the reports for accuracy. An incident narrative should always be included on the form (Johns and Keenan 1997).

School personnel should always inform the parents of all students involved — perpetrators and victims — regarding the incident or situation, and any legal action the school has taken.

Follow state and federal confidentiality laws so no more information other than what is absolutely necessary needs to be given. However, the parent of the victim has the right to know what happened to his/her child.

Police officers, whether placed in a school or called to assist when a crime is committed, must also receive training from school district personnel, particularly in the area of understanding students with disabilities and their particular needs. McAfee and colleagues (2000) point out that police training falls short in addressing issues of violent crime involving students with disabilities. It is critical that the school or the district offers to train police in this regard, according to the researchers. They identified five critical areas of need for police training:

1. Characteristics of juveniles who have disabilities.

2. Violence management within the schools.

3. Legal status of students with disabilities.

4. Procedures for working with mental health agencies and working collaboratively with school personnel.

5. Appropriate documentation of encounters with students with disabilities.

(McAfee and colleagues 2000 p. 19.)

Police officers can be extremely helpful in providing staff development for school personnel. They can provide training on such issues as the legal parameters for crime (what is and what isn't a crime) and police officers (what they can and can't do).

The relationship between the school and the police agency can range from formal to informal, but it will likely have elements of both. As an example of a formal element, police representatives can and should sit on a local school coordinating council. An example of an informal element might be designating a police officer to whom the school can contact for answers to questions, program requests, advice on policies and procedures, and many other issues that may come up in the day-to-day operations of a school (Johns and Keenan 1997).

Districts should establish a local school coordinating council in which the school, police, probation department, state's attorney, and other community agencies work together to ensure that all agencies understand each other's limitations and capabilities. A coordinating council is an excellent communication vehicle that enhances an understanding of the limitations and capabilities of each agency (Johns, Carr and Hoots 1997).

I established a coordinating council in a previous school, and the benefits were tremendous. Each of the agencies got to know what the other agencies did and benefited from the expertise of each. Through a number of measures, our coordinating council tackled the city's truancy problem. When gang problems increased, the police department would meet once a month at 7 a.m. with school personnel from all over the city, along with the probation department. The purpose of the meeting was to give participants ideas for spotting and addressing gang signs and drug paraphernalia, among other issues.

Every school district should prepare a list of what constitutes criminal behavior in their area for administrators and teachers. Each district also must have written policies on the use of police intervention, and those policies should be thoroughly explained to students, families and staff.

Johns and Keenan (1997) have provided guidelines for schools working with the police when pressing criminal charges:

1. Designate a specific staff member as the contact person for police, state attorney's office, and the probation department.

2. Only press charges for true criminal situations and preferably those instances for which there is an adult witness.

3. Before contacting the police about a crime, the staff member who is the police contact should talk with the adult witness or witnesses to verify the incident and the willingness of the witness to testify about the behavior observed.

4. The staff member also should talk with the alleged perpetrator to listen to his or her side of the issue and should provide the alleged perpetrator with fair treatment.

5. The staff member should call police and preferably press charges on behalf of the school so that the victim is less likely to suffer retaliation or fear. The staff member will need to be able to provide the following data about the perpetrator to the police — name, age, date of birth, and parents' address and phone number.

6. The staff member should document the incident, along with the actions the school and police have taken.

7. The staff member must inform the parents of all students involved in an incident and explain the actions the school has taken.

Cautions in the Use of Police Intervention

1. Prior to using police intervention, it is critical to establish a positive working relationship with the police department in order to develop related policies and procedures. Police involvement in policy development and training staff keeps everyone in the loop. This prevents school personnel from calling police for non-criminal actions and prepares both sides for the smooth handling of criminal incidents that do require police intervention.

2. Avoid allowing multiple individuals within the school to call the police for criminal charges. School personnel must designate the individual or few individuals who will represent the school district in making the calls when a criminal act has been committed.

3. Prior to contacting the police about a crime on campus, the staff member who is the designated police contact should talk with the adult witness or witnesses to verify the actual incident and the willingness of the witnesses to testify about the behavior of the perpetrator. At times, the witness will report seeing a criminal act, but when questioned further may change his/her story or not remember who actually did what. Some staff members may become nervous about giving the police information or may not want to get the student in trouble and will therefore change the story.

4. School personnel should be very cautious when using students as witnesses for criminal events. While it is not always possible, it is preferable to rely on adult witnesses. Student witnesses may be afraid of retaliation from the perpetrator. In some jurisdictions, the school is able to press charges on behalf of the victim, avoiding the risk of retaliation against student victims. Ask the local police department if the school can press charges on behalf of the student.

5. School personnel must know exactly where a crime was committed in order to determine appropriate jurisdiction of police departments. This is especially critical for incidents that may occur on the school bus. A fight may have broken out on the bus home from school. The school bus may have been in a different city or county when the actual crime was committed, and, therefore, the police department where the school district is located does not have jurisdiction over the event. The first question an administrator must ask the bus driver in such an event is where the incident occurred.

6. Jurisdiction over an event also may be a problem when a student has run away from school. As soon as a student does run away from school, school personnel must notify the police and the parents. School staff members have a responsibility to keep students safe at school, so they must conduct those notifications. They also must be prepared to provide details on which way the student was heading and provide a brief description of the student. Since student safety is at stake, it's important to provide other critical information — where the student may be going, whether the student is suicidal or homicidal, whether the student is able to perceive a dangerous situation.

As a school administrator, I knew a student who was integrated into a class at another school building within the same city. The student had significant mental retardation and did not see danger. He also had significant problems communicating his needs to others. One day he ran away from the school in which he was integrated. My school had rules on police intervention; the other school did not. One of their staff members went out chasing him, only to discover that the student could run faster than she could. She finally gave up and returned, out of breath, to the school. The receiving school therefore called me, as the administrator from the sending school. From that call, I gathered as much information as I could about where the student was headed and what had happened that might have precipitated the event. The other school did not wish to call the police. I did so as soon as I hung up the phone. I also called the parent.

In this incident, it would have been preferred if the receiving school had directly called the police department, the parent and then me. Valuable time was lost, and a lesson was learned the hard way. The student was found about an hour later. I then worked with the school to determine a contingency plan if such an incident were to occur again and assisted the school in establishing a plan for students who run away.

7. Educators must be very cautious that students do not commit criminal acts so that they get sent to the police department and therefore get out of school. When possible — and when it can be worked out with the police department — consider having the police take the student to the department, book the student for the criminal behavior, and then return the student to school.

8. Police intervention alone will not ensure safety in the schools. Schools must take a series of positive and proactive steps to make sure that students learn appropriate behaviors, are reinforced for the appropriate behaviors, and understand that logical consequences, including police intervention, will be the result for inappropriate behaviors.

9. Educators must teach children which behaviors constitute criminal behavior and that significant consequences result when criminal behavior occurs at school — this is part of the teaching and learning process.

References

Chester Upland (PA) Schools, 24 IDELR 79 (OCR 1995).

Johns, B. and Keenan, J. (1997). *Techniques for managing a safe school.* Denver: Love Publishing.

Johns, B.; Carr, V.; and Hoots, C. (1997). *Reduction of School Violence: Alternatives to Suspension.* Second edition. Horsham, PA: LRP Publications.

McAfee, J. (2000). Policing, school violence, and students with disabilities. *Reaching Today's Youth*, 5(1), 18-21.

SmartStart: Discipline under Section 504. *Special Ed Connection*™ (*www.specialedconnection.com*) (2002). Horsham, PA: LRP Publications.

Intervention #5 – Point Systems

Scenarios

Properly Implementing a Point System

Mrs. Edwards wants to utilize a point system for her instructional class for students with emotional disturbance (ED). Her students are 7 and 8 years old. She reviews their records and notes that the teacher who had the students last year had them on a point system based on the rules of the classroom. Students received one point for each 30-minute block of time for each rule followed. She notes that the students did not get many points. She also notices that there are no behavioral intervention plans (BIPs) for her students. She does find that there were functional assessments conducted. She talks with her special education supervisor and building principal and requests that IEPs be convened for her students. IEPs are scheduled and at the first IEP for Jamie, the team discusses the results of the functional assessment and establishes target behaviors appropriate for Jamie. The major target behavior for, Jamie, an 8-year-old diagnosed with ED, is his failure to complete his written assignments. Through the functional assessment, it was determined that the work given to Jamie is at the appropriate level, but Jamie does not want to do the assignments. Replacement behavior is written work completion. A number of interventions are decided upon — reducing the amount of work that is given to Jamie at one time, choices built into assignments, and the Premack Principle (see p. 17), that when Jamie works independently at a task for five minutes he is allowed to work for two minutes on a preferred activity. The IEP team decides that a point system would be appropriate for Jamie. They determine that the classroom rules will be utilized on the point system — raising hand prior to speaking, keeping hands and feet to self, and respecting the property of others — and that Jamie has no problem following these rules so he should be able to earn points for these behaviors most of the time. The team then determines that the target behavior — work completion — should be part of the point system. Discussion then occurs about the point system time interval that is appropriate for Jamie. The team decides that Jamie needs to be provided a point for each behavior every five minutes. Verbal positive reinforcement will be paired with the awarding of points. The team determines that once points are earned, they will not be removed. They also determine that five bonus points should be given when Jamie completes an assignment ahead of schedule. Jamie likes a variety of reinforcers — time to draw, time to utilize the computer for an educational game, baseball games, and he also likes those little bottles of shampoo that are obtained in hotels. Jamie can earn a total of four points for every five minutes. He can earn up to 24 points every half-hour and 48 points every hour. At the end of every five minutes, Mrs. Edwards asks Jamie to evaluate how he thinks he has done. She then provides her input. She finds that Jamie is very honest and is able to critique his own behavior. Points will be able to be cashed in at the end of each day, and Jamie is given a reinforcer menu — he can either keep his points and build them up or cash them in using the menu.

The IEP team for each individual student meets and determines what is appropriate for the other students in the class. Mrs. Edwards monitors closely the point systems for each of the students within her class and finds them to be working. Since Jamie's point system is working well for a semester, she requests another IEP review to discuss whether it is appropriate to increase the time interval for awarding Jamie's points.

Mrs. Edwards engaged the IEP team in the decision-making process to determine that a point system was an effective intervention for Jamie. The point system was outlined as a behavioral intervention. The time intervals for the points were determined by the team as were the reinforcers. The decision was made to not utilize response cost — taking away points once they are earned. The parent was supportive of the system because she had been involved in the planning.

Now let's look at this scenario.

Improperly Implementing a Point System

Mr. Johns is an instructor in a high school instructional class for eight BD students. He develops a point system for his students based on the rules of his classroom. He puts his rules on the left-hand side of the sheet and breaks down the day into one-hour intervals at which time points will be awarded. At the end of the week he allows the stu-

dents to cash in their points for free time. He determines that the aide will keep track of the points; so the aide carries a clipboard with her at all times to note the points that the students are receiving. If they are misbehaving, she deducts a point for each instance of misbehavior.

What's wrong with this picture? First of all, Mr. Johns is not providing feedback to the students on their behavior. The aide is giving the points but is not pairing the awarding of points with verbal positive reinforcement. The point system does not address the individual target behaviors for each student. The point system is broken down into one-hour intervals. Some of the students in this class may not be able to wait one hour to receive feedback. Points can be cashed in for free time, however, free time may not be motivating to all of the students, in fact it may be a time that some students may spend getting into trouble. The educator would have found it more beneficial to have a menu of rewards from which the students could choose. Lastly, there are no provisions for what will occur if the students "go in the hole" because they have lost so many points.

Definition of Point Systems

Point systems are a form of token reinforcement whereby points are given as tokens for appropriate behavior.

Token reinforcement systems are a contingency package whereby the points are earned as soon as possible following the emission of a target appropriate response and later can be exchanged for a reinforcing object or event (Sulzer-Azaroff and Mayer 1977). Target behaviors are defined and then time intervals are typically utilized to mark down whether the points were earned. As an example, the teacher might make a chart for the student with the target behaviors written down on the left side of the sheet. Time intervals or activity intervals are then broken down across the top of the sheet. The teacher marks down the number of points that are earned during that interval. Target behaviors may include the classroom rules, and for special education students should include the behavioral goals specified in the student's IEP. As an example, target behaviors might include: speak only with permission, keep hands to self, stay on task, follow teacher's directions (these are the classroom rules), and speak in an appropriate tone of voice, and use acceptable language (these are the student's IEP goals). The teacher would instruct the student on what each of these behavioral expectations are.

Correct Use of Point Systems

For younger students, or for students who have developmental disabilities, the teacher may create a point sheet for each student with that student's target behavior; limiting the point system to only one behavior. Point systems for older students may include several behaviors, but should not include too many, otherwise the student may feel overwhelmed.

The educator must carefully select the target behaviors. As stated previously, these may include the classroom rules and should definitely include the individual targeted behaviors outlined on the special education student's IEP. A discussion of those targeted behaviors is an integral part of the functional assessment and behavioral intervention plan.

Zimmerman (2001) suggests that if utilizing several goals or target behaviors on the point sheet, the student should be able to do two of the five goals on a chart and the remaining three can be more challenging. This assures that the student will get some of the points and will meet with some success. She also stresses the importance of reviewing the chart with the student at the end of the time period or at the end of the activity. This helps the student to more easily transition to the next activity.

The target behaviors should be specific, observable, and desired behaviors. Such behaviors as: "Raise your hand and wait for the teacher to call on you before you speak" is an observable and desirable behavior.

Time intervals are critical in the effectiveness of any point system. This author has seen 45-minute time intervals for the rewarding of points to a primary-age student. This is too long of a time interval, especially at the beginning of the implementation of a point system. Young children and students with developmental disabilities need rewards given frequently, and they need feedback as quickly as it can be given. The teacher may want to establish a time interval of five minutes for younger students. Some teachers have chosen to utilize intervals based on activities rather than specific times. As an example, the teacher might break the point system into a reading period, a math period, a social studies period, or lunchtime, etc. Teachers must be certain that the student(s) can wait that long for feedback.

Verbal positive reinforcement should always be paired with the awarding of point systems because the goal is to eventually fade out of the points system and continue giving verbal reinforcement for positive behavior. As Walker, Colvin and Ramsey (1995) point out, consistently recognizing and noting the student's behavior is the most important component of a system. "The rewards will only get a child going; eventually, these new behaviors will become a part of the child's own repertoire of behavior" (Walker, Colvin and Ramsey 1995, p. 289).

A reward menu also must accompany the point system along with the times that the student may "cash-in" points. A reward menu provides the child with choices, such as desired activities or desired objects (a variety of pens and pencils, for instance). It might include self-care items such as little bottles of shampoo, or it might include food (be cautious in today's era of obesity to provide healthy foods and not junk items). Whatever is included should be economical and should consider the interests and desires of the students. Students have to be motivated to earn the items. Obviously more valuable items are utilized for more points.

This author found that some students would choose not to cash in their points for long intervals. Some students are motivated by building up their points and by having more points than anyone else in the class. Hopefully these students will grow up to be good money savers.

When the students may "cash-in" points is also a critical decision. Some teachers may allow students to cash in at the end of the week. However, for some students, they may not be able to wait until the end of the week for the rewards, especially when first implementing the system. For younger students, "store" for cashing in points may occur twice a day or once a day. In making this decision the teacher must consider the social/emotional levels, along with the cognitive levels of his/her students.

Point charts can be an excellent way to collect data and show student improvement or lack of improvement. If the student is not making progress on the point system, then there must be a careful review of the program.

Self-monitoring point systems have been implemented by some educators. Goals are established for the student, and a time or period interval is determined. The student is given his/her own point sheet and at the end of the time or period interval, the student assesses whether he or she has met the goals and therefore earned a point for each goal or target behavior.

Some educators utilize zeros when students do not get the points. If the student has a day with no zeros, then that student receives some type of special recognition.

Bonus points also can be utilized. I always found those to be very effective. For instance, if a student ignores another student who is acting up that student could receive a bonus point or points.

Jones, Dohrn and Dunn (2004) list these advantages of point systems. Point systems provide a clear structure for the student where behaviors will be responded to in fair, rational, and consistent ways and teach students that they will be held accountable for their behavior. A second benefit is that such a system may restore students' lost hope. A point system allows a student to see clear cause and effect relationship between their positive behaviors and the privileges that they earn. A third benefit is to provide adults with a clear structure for reinforcing and reprimanding students. A point system can provide a structure that increases the likelihood that the educator will give positive reinforcement to the student.

Cautions in the Use of Point Systems

1. Be very cautious in the utilization of response cost — a procedure whereby points that already have been earned are taken away when inappropriate behavior occurs. For years, this procedure has been very controversial. There are those who believe that once a student has earned something, it should not be taken away from him or her. There are others that believe it can be used as an appropriate intervention for a student. Some individuals liken response cost to a fine that someone would pay if they violated a given law. Response cost can be effectively utilized, however, there are indeed cautions. The biggest caution is that the educator will start taking away points and the student's behavior will escalate.

The student may yell out: "Who cares, take all my points away." The educator then takes even more points away and soon the student is "in the hole." This author has seen this procedure used incorrectly when the educator keeps taking points away and the student ends up 100 points in the hole. The student feels defeated and gives up because he or she knows it will be very difficult to get out of the hole. Incidentally if that ever happens to an educator, the one thing that can be done to remedy the situation is to give bonus points for appropriate behavior. However the educator should avoid getting into this situation. Sulzer-Azaroff and Mayer (1977) list the advantages of response cost as: strong and rapid behavioral reduction, possible long-lasting effects, and a convenient approach. Among the disadvantages they list include: the danger of using penalties that are too large; the fact that it is an aversive, and because it is an aversive, it may generate escape and aggressive behaviors. These authors recommend a variation of response cost known as bonus response cost. Rather than taking points away that a student has earned, the educator can set up a bonus pool of points. Each day the students are given 10 bonus points at the beginning of the day. If the student misbehaves, it is a predetermined number of those bonus points that are taken away.

2. If the time intervals for the actual point system are too long, the student may give up or may not be able to wait for reinforcement. As an example, the teacher has decided to award points every 50 minutes. However the child is a second-grader and more than likely 50 minutes is much too long for the student to receive feedback on whether he or she is receiving points. This is one of the major flaws this author has seen in point systems — the time interval is too long for the individual student. A time interval plan and its duration should be discussed and determined during the student's IEP meeting and included in the student's BIP.

3. If the time established for cashing in on the points is too long, the system may fail. Some educators establish a weekly

"store" time for the students to buy items with their points; yet some students cannot wait a week to buy items.

4. It is important that, for special education students, that the point system be individualized rather than a "one-size-fits-all" approach for all the students in the class. As recommended before, it is permissive to have some of the target behaviors be the same for all of the students within the class, but there also should be individualized target behaviors based on discussion within the IEP.

5. If skill deficits are targeted on the point system, the educator must provide instruction in those deficit areas. A skill deficit refers to a target behavior that the student has not yet learned. A performance deficit is a behavior that is currently exhibited by the student, but not at a satisfactory criteria. If the teacher is not sure whether the student has a skill deficit or a performance deficit, he or she should assume it is a skill deficit and teach the skill (Johns, Crowley and Guetzloe 2002). Social skills assessments and observational recordings should be utilized to determine whether the student has a skill deficit or performance deficit (Scheuermann and Webber 1996).

6. Educators must be cognizant that the process should not become mechanical. At times, this author has been in schools and seen educators and paraprofessionals carrying around their clipboards and marking points. They are not providing constructive feedback to the student, and they are not pairing the awarding of points with positive verbal reinforcement for the student.

7. Point systems are based on the premise that the student will be able to "cash-in" the points for a reward or rewards. The rewards should be based on the interests and functioning level of the student. The IEP is the excellent vehicle for learning what is motivating to the student; the parent(s) knows what the student likes and how the student likes to spend his or her free time. Motivators should be identified on the IEP. (Johns, Crowley and Guetzloe 2002.) If the motivators are not appro-

priate for the student or are not desirable for the student, then the point system will not be effective.

References

Johns, B., Crowley, E., and Guetzloe, E. (2002). *Effective curriculum for students with Emotional and behavioral disorders*. Denver: Love Publishing.

Jones, V., Dohrn, E., and Dunn, C. (2004). *Creating effective programs for students with emotional and behavior disorders*. Boston: Pearson.

Scheuermann, B., and Webber, J. (1996). Level systems: problems and solutions. *Beyond Behavior*, 7(2), 12-17.

Sulzer-Azaroff, B. and Mayer, G. (1977). *Applying behavior-analysis procedures with children and youth*. New York: Holt, Rinehart, and Winston.

Walker, H., Colvin, G. and Ramsey, E. (1995). *Antisocial behavior in school: strategies and best practices*. Pacific Grove, Ca: Brooks/Cole.

Zimmerman, B. (2001). *Why can't they just behave? a guide to managing student behavior disorders*. Horsham, PA: LRP Publications.

Intervention #6 – Level Systems

Scenarios

Establishing an Effective Level System

Mr. Brown takes a job as a teacher of a cross-categorical class at the high school. Most of his students will be with him for their instruction 80 percent of the time because of the significance of their disabilities. Seven of his eight students have behavioral issues. He is interested in researching how level systems could be utilized within his class. He has read some information about the systems and knows several precautions that he must take. He discusses the use of the level system with his supervisor, and they decide that new IEPs should be convened before any such system is implemented. Last year's teacher had not used a level system and there is no mention of such a system on any of the students' behavioral intervention plans. He is also very concerned that the teachers at the school seem to be very reluctant to accept some of his students in their classes. They are especially resistant to having Willy in any of their classes and grew very tired of him last year being in the hallway bothering their classes. Mr. Brown wants to change that and get his students out of his classroom and into regular classes more. An IEP is convened for Willy. He is having the most significant behavioral issues in the classroom. Willy's target behaviors are determined to be: arriving at school on time and remaining in the classroom unless permission is given to be out of the classroom. The functional assessment determined that Willy's behaviors are attention getting. When he arrives late at school, his mother, the principal, and his teacher become upset and give him negative attention. Willy only lives a block away from school and does not require any special transportation. When he leaves the classroom without permission, the other students think it is funny and laugh. He then wanders the hall and causes disruptions to the entire school.

It is determined by the IEP team that a level system will be appropriate for Willy. Willy is involved in the decision and when asked what he wants to work toward, he replies that he wants more freedom in the school and wants to be able to earn time to go to the gym to shoot baskets. The two target behaviors will be part of the level system as well as the teacher's rules that students stay on task while in the classroom and that students keep their hands and feet to themselves. It is determined that the level system will consist of four levels. Willy will start at Level 1 where the expected behaviors are those that have been delineated above. He will be allowed 10 minutes of free time within the classroom. He is also able to use his Walkman to listen to acceptable music while he is working. It is determined that when Willy meets the target behaviors for five days (not necessarily consecutive days), he will then move to Level 2. At Level 2, Willy will have the privilege of having a five minute break outside the classroom, the ability to go to lunch five minutes early, plus the free time and the use of the Walkman. If Willy complies by following the rules and meeting his target behavior for five more days (again not necessarily consecutively), he will be able to move to Level 3. At Level 3 he will receive a 15-minute time to shoot baskets in the gym, plus he will be able to use his Walkman. When he has complied with the behaviors for seven days on Level 3, he will be given a 20 minute time to shoot baskets and will be able to run errands for the teacher — taking messages to the office — provided he goes and comes back within the specified time frame. He will then move to Level 4 where a new IEP will be convened to determine whether Willy is ready to be integrated into a regular education class; plus Willy will be given four passes that will entitle him to five minutes free time for an acceptable activity of his choice — shooting baskets, free time in the classroom, going to the office to spend positive time with the assistant principal, or spending some positive time talking with the custodian. It is also determined that Mr. Brown should be providing as much positive attention to Willy when he does come to school on time and stays in the classroom. It is also determined that Mr. Brown will call Willy's mother and father twice a week to report on Willy's progress. It is determined that Willy will not drop levels for misbehavior, instead, he will just not move on the level system that day. Mr. Brown makes a chart for Willy to keep on his desk and also teaches him how he can keep track of his level in a computer program. Willy responds well to this system.

Mr. Brown established a level system as determined by the IEP team. His goal was to improve the behavior of Willy and to provide opportunities for Willy to spend increasing time outside his class-room.

Now let's look at this example.

Establishing an Ineffective Level System

Mrs. Swain has decided that she is going to utilize a level system for her sixth-grade class of students with emotional/behavioral disorders. There is no mention of a level system on any of the students' IEPs. She taught the class last year and had problems with behavior management of her students. She establishes a level system — the same for all of the students. She begins all students at Level 1. The behaviors that they must follow are the rules for the classroom. They must meet the behaviors for at least 15 days in a row before moving to Level 2. At Level 1, they must eat lunch in the classroom and cannot have PE. At Level 2, the students are allowed to eat lunch in the cafeteria and can participate in the school's breakfast program. They must comply with the rules for 20 days in a row at Level 2. At Level 3, they are allowed to go to PE along with the other privileges. They proceed to Level 4 if they have met the requirements of Level 3 for 20 days in a row. At Level 4, they are allowed to go to two regular education classes. If a student becomes disruptive in the classroom and starts swearing at her, she drops their level back to Level 1. When her supervisor observes her, he notes that 50 percent of her comments to the students are negative. He also noted that she needed to be providing social skills training for her students. In January, Mrs. Swain is upset because none of the students have moved beyond Level 1.

There are several problems with Mrs. Swains' use of the level system. First of all, she made all the decisions outside the IEP process. She also denied her students' access to a physical education class, which was one of the regular education classes in which her students were to participate. She also denied access to the school's breakfast program, which was provided to all students. In fact, some of the parents were under the impression that their children were receiving the school breakfast program. The teacher also determined regular education classes were contingent on behavior. She made those decisions unilaterally rather than through the IEP process. She did not focus on the individual target behaviors of the students, but instead set up a system that was the same for all the students. Fifteen to twenty days consecutively is a long time for even a student who isn't struggling with behavioral problems to maintain excellent behavior. Mrs. Swain was not assisting her students in succeeding; she needed to provide positive reinforcement when the students were behaving, and she needed to teach the students appropriate social skills. She had engaged in a vicious cycle that was promoting negative behavior rather than encouraging the success of her students.

Definition of Level Systems

Level systems are defined as a hierarchy of behaviors and privileges through which students must progress. Students who engage in a prescribed set of behaviors for a specific number of days earn more privileges the higher they climb on the level system. It can be thought of as a ladder with certain behaviors required on each step of the ladder. At each step of the ladder there are also privileges that the student can earn. Some level systems have equal size steps on the ladder, while there may be some teachers who design larger steps on the ladder, the higher the student progresses.

According to Scheuermann and colleagues (1994), most level systems incorporate a token economy and some also utilize a response-cost component where a student loses a level as punishment for an inappropriate behavior.

Level systems may have as many points on the ladder as the teacher determines. For instance, some teachers may utilize four levels or five levels. A set of behaviors are provided for students — such as, school attendance, compliance with staff directions, appropriate behavior on the bus. Students must meet a set of criteria for those behaviors. As an example at Level O, the student has to meet the criteria at 90 percent for 20 days. While at that level, the student has few privileges — he has to eat lunch within the classroom and is allowed no free time. When the student meets the criteria, the student then moves to Level 1 where he has to meet the criteria at 90 percent for 20 days also. At this level, he is now allowed 10 minutes of free activity during the day and he can eat lunch in the cafeteria. He also can have a morning snack. At Level 2, the student meets the criteria as in the previous levels and can then earn, in addition to the other privileges,

20 minutes of free time and can utilize the school snack machine. At Level 3, the student has to meet the criteria established for 30 days — at this level the student is able to utilize headphones to listen to music while he or she is working, utilize the computer for certain assignments, plus the other privileges from the other levels. Generally with level systems, teachers also establish criteria where a student can "drop a level." Other teachers determine that if certain behaviors occur, the student will move back to Level 0.

Level systems are found in many classrooms for students with emotional/behavioral disorders; although the extent of their use is not really known because there is little research on this topic. They are found more commonly in alternative schools. They may also be found in other special education instructional classrooms. Occasionally they are found in general education classroom, but not often because of the complexity in administering the system and tracking the progress of each student through the levels.

Correct Use of Level Systems

For special education students, a level system as an appropriate behavioral intervention should be discussed and determined in the IEP as part of the behavioral intervention plan. If it is determined to be an appropriate intervention, the IEP team should determine the level at which the student should begin. A system where all students enter the system at the same point does not provide individualization for the student. Many teachers who utilize level systems do so because it is usually applied uniformly to all students; however, the ease of administration of standardized level systems may interfere with individualized instruction for students (Johns et al. 1996). As staff design level systems, they must maintain the individualization of the system within the classroom system. This must be done through the IEP process. Entry level on the system should be determined via the IEP.

How long the student must remain on one level prior to moving to the next level should also be discussed in the IEP meeting. The team must determine the realistic timelines for a student. While some individuals develop level systems that specify that a student has to maintain the behaviors expected on Level 2 for 10 days, this may be much too long for the particular student who is unable to delay gratification that long or who does not understand the concept of time.

Behaviors that are part of the level system should be based on classroom expectations AND the individual target behaviors that are designated within the IEP. As an example, the teacher might have a set of five classroom expectations — such as arriving to class on time, following teacher direction, respecting other students, respecting property, and completing work. The IEP team also may have identified the specific target behaviors appropriate for the particular student as: increasing the use of appropriate language and beginning a task with one teacher reminder.

A key to the success of any level system is the choice of privileges that are earned at each level. As an example, headphones to listen to music might be motivating to some students, but others could care less about this — they will just wait until they get home to listen to the music.

Targeting self-management skills in the level system is critical to its success and to being able to eventually fade out the use of the level system. As an example, if a student's target behavior is on-task behavior, then a system for the student to be able to self-monitor his/her on-task behavior should be built into the student's program.

Jones, Dohrn, and Dunn (2004) have provided a list of components that must be included in both points and level systems. These include: a form that lists the specific and observable behaviors, the time frame for providing feedback, the continuum of levels with the specific criteria for moving up or down on the level system, reinforcers and consequences for each level, and a procedure for ongoing system evaluation.

Johns, Crowley and Guetzloe (2002) have provided this checklist for educators to utilize to evaluate a level system:

1. Is integration into the regular education classroom determined by the IEP team; rather than progression on the level system?

2. Has the IEP team determined the entry level for the student on the level system?

3. Is placement on the level system based on adequa evaluation?

4. Are skill and performance deficits considered wh.... .... oping the target behaviors on the level system? Are there procedures in place to address those skill and performance deficits?

5. Does each student have individually determined target behaviors based on the IEP goals of the student?

6. Are reinforcers individually determined?

7. Are advancement criteria appropriate for each student and based on the student's developmental level?

8. Is each student's progress on the level system monitored on a regular basis and a new IEP convened when there is a lack of progress?

9. Are self-management strategies incorporated into the level system?

10. Do behaviors that are addressed in the level system maintain over a period of time and generalize to other settings?

Cautions in the Use of Level Systems

1. Level systems should not determine access to general education classes. The law is specific that it is the IEP team who determines the extent of that access. Educational placement and access to nondisabled peers cannot be used as a level system privilege. An option for educators developing level systems is to state that when a student reaches a certain level, a new IEP will be convened for purposes of determining change in placement — an increase in general education time.

2. Students should not be expected to attain the same behaviors at the same mastery criteria and schedule. One student may have a different skill level than another student. Criteria for progressing through the level system should be addressed individually. It is not appropriate for all students within the

67

class to enter the level system at the same level — the decision for the appropriate level for entrance into the level system should be made by the IEP team (Johns, Crowley and Guetzloe 2002).

3. Privileges should not be arranged hierarchically with those most desired by the individual student only at the top. The student may give up because he or she cannot postpone gratification.

4. Reinforcers must be considered individually for the student. Educators should never assume that reinforcers will be the same for all students within the classroom — free time for computer use for educational games may be appropriate for one student but may not be for another student who would rather have free time to read a book.

5. Consequences for not complying with the level system requirements also should be individually determined. Some educators establish level systems where a major behavioral incident such as swearing at the teacher results in a drop to Day 1, Level 1 of the level system. This may be too harsh of a consequence for some students. The details of the consequences should be discussed and delineated in the IEP process.

6. The IEP team should not only determine whether a level system may be an appropriate behavioral intervention for a student, but they also should determine whether the student is making satisfactory progress through the level system. If the IEP team has determined that the student will enter the level system at Level 1 and a grading period later, the student has not moved from Level 1, the team should be investigating whether the system is an appropriate intervention for the student or whether the system is set up appropriately for the individual student.

7. Just as in the execution of point systems, if skill deficits are targeted on the level system, the educator must provide instruction in those deficit areas. A skill deficit refers to a tar-

get behavior that the student has not yet learned. A performance deficit is a behavior that is currently exhibited by the student but not at a satisfactory criteria. If the teacher is not sure whether the student has a skill deficit or a performance deficit, he or she should assume it is a skill deficit and teach the skill (Johns, Crowley and Guetzloe 2002).

8. Educators must be very cautious about the public display of the particular levels of each student. First of all, a student who does not progress in the level system may be ridiculed by other students. A student who is "head of the class" may brag about that fact to the other students, and the other students may become resentful. The public display of the level system may violate the student's right to privacy. One parent may come in and note the levels of the other students; visitors may do the same thing. If the level system is individualized as it should be, the levels should not be competitive; but rather based on the progress of the individual student. Therefore the student's progress on the level system may be noted at the student's desk.

References

Johns, B., Crowley, E., and Guetzloe, E. (2002). *Effective curriculum for students with emotional and behavioral disorders*. Denver: Love Publishing.

Johns, B., Guetzloe, E., Yell, M., Scheuermann, B., Webber, J., Carr, V. and Smith, C.(1996). *Best practices for managing adolescents with emotional/behavioral disorders within the school environment*.

Jones, V., Dohrn, E., and Dunn, C. (2004). *Creating effective programs for students with emotional and behavior disorders*. Boston: Pearson.

Scheuermann, B., Webber, J., Partin, M., and Knies, W. (1994). Level systems and the law: are they compatible? *Behavioral Disorders*, 19(3), 205-220.

Intervention #7 - Study Carrels

Scenarios

Appropriate Use of a Study Carrel

Tyrone is easily frustrated with timed tasks. He gets particularly upset when he sees someone finish an assignment before he can complete it. Mrs. Walsh has been working with him to practice timed tasks and stressing the importance of doing his best. Tyrone has a math test coming up, and Mrs. Walsh determines that allowing Tyrone to take the math test in the study carrel may help reduce his anxiety. Mrs. Walsh is allowing Tyrone to use the study carrel for a specific purpose: She is working to teach him how to take timed tasks and build his self-confidence in those types of assignments. This is an appropriate use of a study carrel.

Inappropriate Use of a Study Carrel

Jeremy can be very disruptive in Mrs. Stallings' sixth-grade classroom. Mrs. Stallings has become increasingly aggravated with Jeremy's behavior. She decides to request a study carrel from the office and puts it in a corner of the classroom. She assigns Jeremy to the study carrel as his permanent desk. When students are doing group activities, Jeremy has to stay in his study carrel. When students are doing individual activities, Jeremy remains in the study carrel. Mrs. Stallings informs Jeremy that he has to use the study carrel until his behavior improves to her satisfaction. However, she does not tell Jeremy what that criterion is. Jeremy's disruptive behavior continues, and he remains there the rest of the year. Jeremy has not learned what is expected of him or how to behave or interact appropriately with his peers.

In another classroom, Marianne has been assigned to a study carrel to do her individual assignments. Rather than doing the assignments, she sleeps or works on the art she loves.

Both of these examples are inappropriate uses of study carrels.

Definition of Study Carrels

A study carrel can be a freestanding desk or a cardboard or wooden stand that can be placed on a desk with three closed sides designed to provide optimum privacy for individual study. It also provides the student with a personal work environment. Examples:

- A freestanding desk with three closed sides, sometimes referred to as a floor carrel.

- A three-sided cardboard stand (purchased or made) that can be placed on a desk to block the view of the working student.

- An old refrigerator box with the top and a side cut out of it, then placed around the student's desk. Some teachers may refer to this as the "student's office." Some schools also use office partitions in this way.

Correct Use of Study Carrels

In elementary and secondary schools, study carrels sometimes are used to reduce distractions for students while they strive to complete independent academic assignments. In the classic textbook, *The Emotionally Disturbed Child in the Classroom*, Frank Hewett (1974), discusses the need for two of these in each instructional class for students with ED. He called them study booths or offices. "The offices are primarily used with students undertaking mastery assignments but who need a more secluded working environment." (p. 242). He cautioned that such study booths are not included in the design of the classroom because of the belief that children with ED are so stimulus-prone that they have to be isolated in sterile surroundings. He believes that reality and environmental stimulation are essential in reducing self-stimulation and fantasy preoccupation that can occur among children with ED who exhibit attention and response problems.

Hewitt further explains that these offices might be carpeted, have nice chairs and contain large tables with screens dividing them. His belief is that "[t]he teacher should attempt to make the specialized work area as glamorous and acceptable as possible for students who are not able to work comfortably on mastery assignments at their regular desks." (pp. 242-243.)

The classroom environment should be a beautiful place to be, so all teachers should work to make sure that the environment is pleasant to the eye. A classroom where students can only work in a study carrel is not such an environment. One or two study carrels should be in each classroom. They can be provided as a choice activity for a student. Again, the more we can empower students, the more likely they will buy into the school program and do the assignments expected of them.

Cautions in the Use of Study Carrels

1. Study carrels should not be the only work area for the student during the day. I have seen teachers overuse carrels by placing students in them the entire day. As a result, the student is not learning social skills and how to work with others.

2. Teachers must supervise students using study carrels. Sometimes, the teacher may think that the student is working on an independent task when in fact the student is drawing gang signs or writing inappropriate statements. The student also may be sleeping or simply not engaged in any learning activity.

3. Students should not be placed in study carrels because the teacher is frustrated with the student's behavior and wants to isolate and ignore the student. Research is showing that teachers teach less to students who exhibit behavioral problems. Students act up, the teacher avoids the student, the student is not taught and the student falls behind academically. Placing a student in a study carrel because the teacher does not want to deal with the student is harmful to the student.

4. Study carrels should not be used as a time-out for a student. As discussed in the time-out intervention segment, time-out is the removal of all opportunity for reinforcement and a very short period of time to regain control. Study carrels are the opportunity for a student to work independently.

References

Hewett, F. (1974). *The Emotionally Disturbed Child in the Classroom*. Boston: Allyn and Bacon.

Intervention #8 - In-School Suspension

Scenarios

An Effective In-School Suspension Plan

Merryville High School has established an in-school suspension program. The school has determined that it will no longer give out-of-school suspensions, and they want to assure that their school keeps students there. A committee made up of parents, educators, school board members, students, representatives of agencies, students, and other interested parties develop a policy that is approved by the school board. As part of the policy, if any student serves 10 days in in-school suspension, an evaluation of whether the program is effective for that student will be conducted. If the student is within special education, a new IEP will be convened. Within the in-school suspension program will be two teachers assigned to monitor the academic work that the students are expected to do. The two teachers assigned to in-school suspension will receive training in the area of behavior management. The school social worker will see each student in the in-school suspension to work on social skills. Special education students will still receive their special education services. The school district will keep data on the students who are using in-school suspension and on the student's resulting specific behaviors. The data will be shared with staff, and increased assistance and training will be provided to classroom teachers on positive ways to deal with the specific behaviors.

In this example, Merryville High School has adopted a program to keep students in school. Widespread input on the program was received by the members of the committee. Policies and procedures were developed for the program. Two teachers were employed for the program, and the necessary training and support were provided to those individuals. Social work services and special education was provided to those students who had IEPs. Ongoing data was collected and analyzed, and changes were made based on that data.

Now let's look at another high school in a neighboring community.

An Ineffective In-School Suspension Plan

Harderville School utilizes in-school suspension. They have desig-nated a room right off the office so the principal and assistant princi-pal can monitor the students. If the principal or assistant principal is gone or is called to an emergency, the school secretary keeps an eye on the students. Some of the students who come to in-school suspen-sion bring work, others bring some but not enough, and others bring no work. Some of the students think it is great fun to be close to the office because it's where the action is. Seventy-five percent of the stu-dents act up and eventually get an out-of school suspension. Others sleep a significant part of the day. What's wrong with this in-school suspension? There are several glaring problems. At times the students are not supervised by an appropriately credentialed individual, for instance the school secretary should not be expected to supervise the students. The principal and assistant principal, because of the many demands of their jobs, also do not have time to take on this task. Some of the students are being reinforced for negative behavior since they actually like to be close to the office where they can see what is hap-pening. Some also like to sleep rather than work. This in-school sus-pension definitely needs to be revisited.

Definition of In-School Suspension

In-school suspension can be defined as the assignment to a super-vised area away from other students where the suspended student does his/her academic work or follows a prescribed curriculum. There are two general approaches to curriculum in an in-school suspension program. One such approach offers a continuation of the student's general education curriculum. This approach requires the coordina-tion of instructions between the in-school suspension teacher/supervi-sor and the general education teacher. The in-school suspension teacher(s) must be familiar with a broad range of curriculum (Johns, Carr and Hoots 1997).

A variation of this type of approach is utilized at Coffeeville High School in Mississippi. Television cameras are installed in each of the classrooms so that students placed in the alternative program can watch their regular classes live on a computer screen from another building. A teacher is assigned to the area to monitor the students (d'Oliveira 2004). This assists students in keeping up with their work and not falling behind. Prior to the system being installed, the students would complain that they did not understand the lessons that were taught by the teachers assigned to the alternative program. This is a solution for schools that encounter having a properly certified teacher instructing a student in a high level course because there are instances where excellent academic students receive an in-school suspension.

The other approach is to develop an in-school suspension curriculum that is able to stand-alone. It could be either a learning skills program, where students study learning strategies or a functional academics program such as daily living or work skills (Johns, Carr and Hoots 1997).

Either approach should include a behavior management segment that provides positive reinforcement to the students for appropriate behavior and work completion.

Correct Use of In-School Suspension

In the *Study of State and Local Implementation and Impact of the Individuals with Disabilities Education Act, Final Interim Report* (1999-2000 School Year), issued in November 2003, it was found that nearly three-fourths of schools had an in-school suspension program during the 1999-2000 school year. The schools also incorporated specific features in their programs. Approximately two-thirds of all the schools that have in-school suspension programs included counseling or support designed to prevent the behavior from happening again, and academic support to help students with assignments from their general education classes. Half of the in-school suspension programs were staffed consistently by the same staff member. In the study it also was noted that in-school suspensions were comparable for both students with disabilities and without disabilities. The study revealed that in-school suspensions of students with disabilities were more common in the West than in the South, Midwest, or Northeast.

There are several promising findings from this study, including the use of counseling or support, academic support to help the students with their assignments, and staff consistency.

The teacher(s) assigned to work in an in-school suspension program must be a highly skilled instructor, be able to utilize positive behavioral interventions, and be able to relate to the students.

Cautions in the Use of In-School Suspension

1. Is an in-school suspension considered a major change in placement for a student? A district must proceed very cautiously. Caruso (2002) advised that if the in-school suspension is equivalent educationally to an out-of-school suspension, it may be. If the school district is simply providing custodial care during the in-school suspension, then it could be a change in placement if it is over 10 days. If the in-school suspension is over 10 days and results in an interruption in the services or educational programming of a student, then it could constitute a change in placement. In *Chester County Tennessee School District*, 17 IDELR 301 (OCR 1990), an in-school suspension program was established. If the student had a disability, the district assigned that student to a classroom with a qualified special educator, and the student continued his coursework in accordance with the IEP. The Office of Civil Rights ruled that the "standard for determining a long-term ISS is a significant change in placement is whether the nature and quality of the services provided to students with disabilities in the program are comparable, in nature and quality, to the educational services they regularly receive" (Caruso 2002).

2. The quality of the in-school suspension must be the same for students with disabilities as those for students without disabilities. In *McCracken County School District*, 18 IDELR 482 (OCR 1991), the district violated Section 504 of the Rehabilitation Act for placing students with disabilities serving in-school suspensions in a poorly lit janitorial supply closet. Further the district provided no adult supervision for some students for several days. This placement also resulted in a change of services for the student and was different for students with disabilities from what occurred with the general

education students. (Richards, *School Discipline Advisor*, 2004).

3. Educators must be very careful that in-school suspension is not where a student prefers to be rather than in the classroom setting. If a student is allowed to sleep or not work, he or she probably will prefer the in-school suspension to the classroom environment. If the student gets more positive attention from the instructor of the in-school suspension program than he/she receives from his/her regular education instructors, then in-school suspension will be a reward.

4. Teachers who supervise the suspension must receive special training on appropriate behavior management, otherwise they will have difficulty dealing with the myriad of behavioral issues that might occur when a group of students who already have been in trouble are put together for an in-school suspension.

5. All teachers must be trained on the appropriate use of in-school suspensions and what will be expected of them when the student is in the suspension area. The teacher will need to provide a clear set of expectations on what work the student is expected to do while in the in-school suspension area and also make sure that there is enough work for the time allotted. And the work should be that which the student can complete independently.

In-school suspension can be a much more productive method of dealing with behavioral challenges than out-of-school suspension. The key to whether it is an effective management strategy lies within its implementation.

References

Caruso, B. (2002). *Discipline and the section 504 student: your quick-reference guide to best practices*. Horsham, PA: LRP Publications.

Chester County (TN) Sch. Dist., 17 IDELR 301 (OCR 1990).

d'Oliveira, S. (2004). Suspended students stay tuned into their school-work computer. *School Discipline Advisor*, 5(12), 1,4.

McCracken County Sch. Dist., 18 IDELR 482 (OCR 1991).

Johns, B., Carr, V., Hoots, C. (1997). *Reduction of school violence: alternatives to suspension.* Horsham, PA: LRP Publications.

Richards, D. (2004). School district policies do not overrule section 504. In d'Oliveira, (Editor), *The School Discipline Advisor*, 6(4), 3.

Schiller, E. et al. (2003). *The study of state and local implementation and impact of the* Individuals with Disabilities Education Act: Final Interim Report (1999-2000 school year*).* Bethesda, Md: Abt Associates, Inc.

Intervention #9 – Detention/Time for Time

The use of detention or time for time can be an effective deterrent for inappropriate behavior or for lack of work completion, if it is executed appropriately. Let's look at the following example.

Scenarios

Detention/Time for Time as an Effective Intervention Strategy

Mrs. Carr's classroom in Jefferson School has a policy where students who fail to complete their given work at school can be kept at school until the work is completed. That policy has been reviewed with the parents. Jefferson School staff are assigned (with compensation) to stay on different days of the week with those students who have work to complete or who have gotten into some type of trouble. The school provides alternate transportation for the students to get home. At Mindy's IEP, this intervention was discussed since Mindy has problems completing her assignments, even though staff have determined that the work is at the appropriate level for her. One day, Mindy does not complete her assignments. The teacher warns Mindy that her work needs to be done before she can go home. She then is told that she will have to stay at school until the work is done. Her teacher calls her mother and tells her what has happened and that she will keep her posted on what time Mindy will be home. Mindy completes her work by 4:30 p.m. and is taken home. Detention/time for time was an effective strategy for Mindy.

Detention/Time for Time as an Ineffective Intervention Strategy

Justin was a 16-year-old student who attended the school in which I was the administrator. The teacher in his class used detention/time for time for the students within her class when the students failed to complete their assignments. For each minute that the students were off task, they had to spend comparable time after school. The students generally would stay and do their work in my office. Justin was staying after school frequently. I suggested to the teacher that another system would be appropriate for Justin, not because I did not want to *have Justin in my office, but because I noticed Justin seemed to <u>want</u> to stay after school. We sat down after school to work out a different system, but the teacher had already told Justin that he had to stay because he had failed to do his work. That evening, I was sitting with Justin. I was doing my work, and he was indeed doing his work. He looked up from his work and said to me, very pitifully, "You know I really like it here." I thought about Justin's life outside of school — he had been physically abused at home, his mother often drank and yelled and screamed at him, he and his mother frequently moved from place to place. He certainly did like our school better than his home. We did not yell or hurt him, we treated him with respect, and we provided a caring environment for him. Time for time did not work for Justin. It was an ineffective strategy. We worked out a system when, if Justin had a good day and completed his work, he could stay after school and do a special activity with the teacher or with me.*

Definition of Detention/Time for Time

Sautner (2001) discriminated between a minor detention and a major detention. She defined a minor detention as: "loss of noon hour/recess privilege coupled with a small work assignment related to the effects of the inappropriate behavior on others." (p. 213). She defined a major detention as "detention after school or over the noon hour for one or more days, loss of free-time privilege for one or more occasions, and a larger work assignment related to developing more effective alternative strategies. (p. 213). A detention/time for time may be utilized because a student refused to do his or her work. It may also be used to make up time that was lost on academic tasks because of inappropriate behavior. The student may have thrown a tantrum and lost a great deal of instructional time and therefore has to stay after school to make up the time lost. Detention/time for time also may be used when a student is tardy or truant to make up the time.

A detention denotes that the student will have to stay after school or lose noon hour or recess privileges, but the time may not necessarily match the amount of time the student was off task, was engaged in inappropriate behavior, or was truant. Time for time denotes that the time will match. As an example, if the student was one hour late for school, then the student will stay for one hour. If the student threw a tantrum and lost one hour of instructional time, then the student would have to make up one hour.

Correct Use of Detention/Time for Time

It is critical that staff use detention or time for time as quickly as possible after the behavior occurs. Some schools have a policy where they will keep students after school to serve detentions only on certain days of the week or 24 hours after the event occurs. The problem with this is that it is not immediate and some students will simply not show up for school on the day that they are to serve the detention. Some schools also have a system where students stay only until a certain time to do their work— for example, 4:30 p.m. This is not as effective as requiring the student to stay until the work is completed. This author has found that, with the majority of students, once students know that such a procedure for making up time is in effect, the number of students who refuse to work diminishes.

When a school decides to use a system where students will stay to complete work or to make up time because of inappropriate behavior, it is critical to establish a policy for its use. Such a procedure must be explained fully to staff, students, and to parents. Staff must be willing to stay after school or to be employed by the school district for time after school. And they must be willing to stay any evening of the week when an incident occurs. In some schools, it may not be safe to stay after school after dark therefore a different system will have to be utilized — detention during lunch period or at recess, for younger students.

The school district also must be prepared to transport the student home when the detention/time for time is completed. While the school may request that the parent pick up his/her child, the school district cannot enforce that. Some parents simply will not pick up their child after school or they cannot. Some parents may not have transportation or may have an unreliable car.

If staff will not or cannot stay after school, then another option might be to deduct time from the student's lunch period or recess, for younger students. Staff still must make sure that students get their lunch within a reasonable lunchtime.

Use of detention/time for time should be evaluated regularly to determine whether it is effective for particular students.

For special education students, the use of detention/time for time should be discussed during the preparation of their behavioral intervention plan (BIP). This may be a logical consequence for work refusal or tardiness or inappropriate behavior, but it should not be used as a stand-alone intervention. Positive interventions must be utilized for work completion, arriving at school on time, or appropriate behavior.

Cautions in the Use of Detention/Time for Time

1. When utilizing this approach, have the student stay and make up the time on the same day in which the behavior occurred. It is much less effective to have students stay a different night other than the day in which the behavior occurred. Some school districts provide the student with a 24-hour notice that they will need to serve a detention. A major problem with that is that the student may not show up for school on the day that he or she is supposed to serve the detention. Some students that are functioning at a lower cognitive level may not understand the relationship between the behavioral occurrence and staying after on a different day.

2. If the school has determined that they will take time away from lunch, they must be very cautious that the student still gets his or her food to eat within a reasonable amount of time. Staff also must be very cautious of specific medical needs of individual students. I heard a story not too long ago where a teacher utilized time for time for her entire class when they did not complete their assignments. One of the students had diabetes and had to eat at specific times. The teacher had to adjust her demands for this student.

3. Determining whether this is an appropriate intervention for a student with a disability should be discussed during the IEP process. Specific procedures for this intervention should be discussed also — should time be taken from recess, should lunch be delayed, should the student stay after school.

4. The procedure should be evaluated on a regular basis to determine whether it is appropriate for a particular student.

5. A critical drawback to using such an intervention arises from students who seek teacher attention and want to stay with the teacher after school or during lunch. These students are actually being socially reinforced when they are spending time after school with the teacher. Likewise, a teacher may decide to keep the student in the classroom during the lunch period as a detention and this, too, may be reinforcing to the student. Staff must observe the student very carefully to determine whether he or she seems happy or sad during this time. The intervention may be reinforcing to the student. To prevent that, assign a staff member that is least reinforcing to the student to supervise the student during this time. Another option is for the teacher to refrain from talking as much as possible to the student. In most cases, if there is a non-reinforcing environment, the student does not want to stay after school or in the classroom during lunch (Johns, Carr and Hoots 1997).

6. Another caution centers around how and if teachers are compensated for staying after school. Some schools designate after-school detention teachers who are compensated for their time. This is certainly ideal. School administrators will need to monitor such a system very cautiously to assure that no teacher is abusing the system of compensation. No one school staff member should ever be left alone with a student; at least two staff members should stay, and it may be appropriate for more staff to stay if it has been determined that the student may become aggressive. Administrators must support staff in the use of this intervention and offer to stay. This author can remember evenings at school with students. Lack of administrative support is aversive to staff and makes staff unwilling to try alternative interventions such as time for time (Johns, Carr and Hoots 1997).

References

Johns, B., Carr, V., and Hoots, C. (1997). *Reduction of school violence: alternatives to suspension.* Horsham, PA: LRP Publications.

Sautner, B. (2001). Rethinking the effectiveness of suspension. *Reclaiming children and youth*, 9(4), 210-214.

Intervention #10 – Removal of Privileges

Scenarios

Removal of Privileges as an Effective Intervention Strategy – Scenario #1

Mrs. Johns has her first-grade students out for a special 15-minute recess because the students have had a great morning and have completed their work. As she gets ready to take them out, she reminds them of her rules — they are to play cooperatively, follow the rules of the game, and share the balls that are being taken out. She reminds the students that if anyone violates the rules they will have to sit out for two minutes. On the playground, Mrs. Johns is watching the students and praising those that are playing cooperatively, sharing the balls, and following the rules of the games they are playing. She then notices that Carey goes up to Samantha who is playing ball with three other children, and without warning, yanks the ball out of Samantha's arms. Mrs. Johns goes up to Carey and tells her to give the ball back to Samantha and that she needs to sit out for two minutes.

In this instance, Mrs. Johns had taken the students out for a special recess. She reviewed the rules with her class and stated the consequences for students who failed to follow the rules. She praised those students who were following the rules. When she observed the inappropriate behavior, she immediately invoked the predetermined consequence. She had the student sit out for a two-minute period of time.

Now let's look at a secondary school example.

Removal of Privileges as an Effective Intervention Strategy – Scenario #2

Sunnyside School has a policy that juniors and seniors who maintain a C or above average and have no unexcused absences or tardies can drive their cars to school. This is a privilege that is earned. The behaviors that result in the loss of the privilege are failure to maintain the C or above average, an unexcused absence, speeding in the parking lot, or having contraband within the car. The first offense results in a loss of driving privileges for one week, the second offense results in the loss for two weeks, and the third offense results in the loss of driving privileges for the remainder of the school year, including the extended school year. This policy was written and adopted by the School Board. A copy of it was provided to parents and students. It was orally reviewed with the students and the staff.

Steve has the privilege of driving his car to school. However one day he is pulling in the parking lot and one of the teachers sees him "showing off" for some of his fellow students by gunning the motor and speeding around the corner into a parking space. The teacher waits for Steve and tells him what she just saw and that she is reporting the incident to the principal. She writes up the incident and turns it in to the Principal. Steve is called into the office and informed that he has lost the privilege of driving his car to school for two weeks.

In this instance, the school had a written policy and enforced the policy. Students knew ahead of time that if they abused the privilege of driving to school, they would lose that privilege for a specified period of time. Furthermore, there were progressive consequences depending on the number of times there were violations of the school policy.

Now let's look at these examples of what *not* to do.

Removal of Privileges as an Ineffective Intervention Strategy

"You have lost your recess for the rest of the year." Mrs. Borne gets mad at Jason while he is out on the playground because he trips another student, and, in her anger, makes this statement to the 6-year-old. Jason becomes angry and figures he already has lost recess for the rest of the year so he might as well "go for broke."

This author remembers an incident in a school district when the students were going on their senior trip. Bill was excited about the senior trip and the upcoming graduation. He was going to be the first family member who ever graduated from high school, and he was so proud of his accomplishments, as was his family. Rules were not established for the field trip. On the way home, students were becoming rowdy on the bus. Bill, from his bus seat, decided to moon someone in a passing car. When the bus returned and the advisor reported the incident to the principal, the principal yelled at Bill: "That's it, you are not graduating from high school." Bill became very angry and ran home and got a gun. He was intent on coming back to school and shooting the principal, however, on the way back to school, he turned the gun on himself and committed suicide.

One might argue that it was certainly not appropriate for Bill to moon someone, but did the punishment fit the inappropriate behavior? Did the students know ahead of time that inappropriate behavior could result in the loss of graduation?

Definition of Removal of Privileges

Sautner (2001) defines the removal of privileges as one when the "student is ineligible for extracurricular groups, field trips, and so forth until behavior shows consistent improvement." (p. 214.) Removal of Privileges may be used as a logical consequence for a student who misbehaves. As an example, Steve was allowed to drive his car to and from school. He was caught speeding in the parking lot at school. That privilege was removed for a period of time as a logical consequence.

Correct Use of Removal of Privileges

Johns, Carr and Hoots (1997) state that the loss of privileges is most effective when the privilege the child loses is a natural or logical consequence of the specific inappropriate behavior. When utilizing the loss of privileges, it is important to utilize these guidelines:

1. Let the student know and be sure the student understands the relationship of the behavior and the lost privilege. For a young child, the adult may state: "Because you would not share the toy with Billy, you cannot play with the toy for two minutes." For an older student, the staff member might say: "Because you misused the computer by writing a personal e-mail to another student, you have lost the privilege of using the computer for two weeks."

2. Be sure that the school has established written and approved policies on the removal of privileges so when an incident occurs, staff has clear guidance on what specific actions to take.

89

3. Be sure the student has been taught the appropriate behavior and the consequences for not following the rule. As an example, the younger student will need to be taught how to share a toy and needs to know that the consequence for not sharing the toy is losing the privilege of playing with the toy for a period of time.

4. Be sure the student is being reinforced positively for the appropriate behavior in which he or she engages. The loss of privileges will not be effective if the student is not recognized when he or she is engaging in appropriate behavior.

5. Assure that loss of privileges is logical. As an example, if the student has inappropriately used the computer, the logical consequence is loss of computer privileges for a period of time, rather than losing recess time.

6. Provide a warning to the student that if he or she engages in a certain behavior, he will lose the privilege. Unfortunately this author has seen school personnel remove a privilege from a student with no warning — as an example, the student has engaged in an inappropriate behavior and the staff member says: "That's it, you are not going on the field trip."

7. It is critical that staff be consistent in the loss of privileges. If policy states that inappropriate use of the computer results in loss of computer privileges for two weeks, then that is the consequence that needs to be given. It is unfair to give one consequence to one student whose father happens to be President of the School Board than to another student who engages in the same behavior.

8. School personnel may want to consider a hierarchy of loss of privileges either for specific incidents or for number of times an incident has occurred. Let's look again at the example of the inappropriate use of the computer. Using a computer for sending a personal e-mail probably should not be as serious as using a computer for accessing pornography. The first time an event occurs may result in a loss of privileges for

a given period of time; the second time an event occurs may result in the loss of privileges for a longer period of time.

9. Assure that the consequence is reasonable for the inappropriate behavior that occurred. Because a student refused to play with another student, it is not appropriate to remove recess privileges for a long period of time. The first time the student engages in such behavior, the teacher might want to remove recess for a short period of time (a few minutes). The teacher should then explore the behavior to ascertain the reason the student did not want to play with the other student.

Cautions in the Use of Loss of Privileges

1. Do not allow students to engage in negotiations on the loss of privileges. As an example, staff have predetermined that the student will lose the use of the computer for inappropriate use for two weeks. The student begs and pleads that he should only lose the use of the computer for one week. Staff feel guilty and give in to the student's request. The student has controlled the situation. An advantage of working out consequences ahead of time and writing them down is that the student cannot negotiate (even though the student will try), and the staff member feels more confident in giving the consequence.

2. Staff should not feel guilty when the child loses a privilege. Provided the student knows the rule and knows the consequence, the student made the choice to break the rule and should definitely lose the privilege. If staff have provided a warning and staff have made it very clear about the consequence, it is important to be fair and consistent and apply the consequence of losing the privilege. Students lose respect for adults who do not follow through with what they say they will do.

3. Be very careful that you do not remove all privileges for a long period of time. In the earlier example where the teacher took recess away from Jason for the rest of the year, Jason

perceived that he had nothing else to lose and so he might as well go ahead and increase his misbehavior.

4. Be very careful that the privileges being removed from the student are ones that are meaningful to the student. While most secondary students would be very upset about losing the privilege of driving a car to school, there may be a few students who don't want to drive — they may be embarrassed by the type of car they have or not feel skilled enough to drive the car. Younger students may not like recess; they would prefer to sit in the classroom and do a quiet activity rather than be physically active.

References

Sautner, B. (2001). Rethinking the effectiveness of suspension. *Reclaiming children and youth*, 9(4), 210-214.

Intervention #11 – Planned Ignoring of Inappropriate Behavior

Scenarios

Let's look at these examples of effective planned ignoring.

Ignoring the Behavior as an Effective Intervention Strategy – Scenario #1

Mrs. Harper is waiting for her first-graders to become quiet prior to reading the students a story. Most of the students have gathered on the carpet area for the story. A few students are slow getting there because they are talking to other students. The teacher ignores these few students and instead praises the students who have already gathered on the carpet — "I really like the way Jill is sitting quietly and waiting to hear the story." "Wow — Bill you walked quietly to the carpet and are ready for the story — thank you." The students who have been taking their time getting to the carpet hurry up to hear the story.

Ignoring the Behavior as an Effective Intervention Strategy – Scenario #2

In a high school English classroom, the students in Mrs. Holden's class have been given an independent writing assignment for which they are to create an outline. Mrs. Holden has instructed the class and provided a sample outline. She then proceeds to walk around the room assisting students. She notes that Craig has his head on his desk and is not working. She ignores him and attends to the students who are working. She then sees Craig lift his head up and begin working. She moves over to Craig and asks if she can assist him. She notes that he has already completed a part of the outline, and she praises what he has done. Both Mrs. Harper and Mrs. Holden used planned ignoring correctly. They ignored behavior that was non-aggressive and non-disruptive and praised appropriate behavior.

Now, picture the following scene.

93

Ignoring the Behavior as an Ineffective Intervention

Mrs. Korey is in the hallway doing duty. She notices that Aaron goes up to Melissa and punches her on the side of her arm. Melissa yells out for Mrs. Korey to do something. Mrs. Korey replies: "Aaron was just kidding." Mrs. Korey then does nothing. The next day Aaron goes up to Melissa and hits her even harder. On this day, Mrs. Korey doesn't want to deal with the problem and just ignores Aaron. This continues over the course of a week, and Melissa goes to the office and complains she has a bruise from Aaron hitting her. This is an example of what type of behavior should never be ignored. Aaron was engaging in aggressive behavior that is not appropriate in the school setting. When Mrs. Korey did not do anything, she was condoning the behavior. Consequently, Aaron's behavior escalated and Melissa was physically hurt in the process. Planned ignoring should never be used for such aggressive behavior.

Definition of Planned Ignoring

Planned ignoring can be defined as ignoring with deliberate intent for the purpose of eliminating a student's undesirable behavior that is being reinforced through teacher attention (Vaughn, Bos and Schumm 1997). Such planned ignoring is also known as extinction. As Vaughn and associates point out, ignoring can be a very effective intervention, but may be impractical for many behaviors that happen in a classroom because the reinforcement for the student's behavior may not be under the teacher's control. As an example, the student might be engaging in "talk-outs." The teacher can ignore the behavior and not attend to the student, but the other students may think it is funny and give him the attention he wants. Peer attention is more important to this student.

Likewise the behavior gets worse before it gets better because the student is "testing the limits" of what he can do. I can remember deciding to ignore a first-grader who was out of her seat. I was doing a good job of ignoring her, as were the other students in the class. She not only got out of her seat, but then proceeded to run around the classroom and then started yelling at me: "What's the matter teacher, can't you hear." The behavior eventually got better, but our class really "weathered a storm" that was very disruptive to me and to the other students. I have known teachers that decided to ignore students who were out of their seats and then the students ran away from the classroom and then left the building.

Correct Use of Planned Ignoring

When determining whether to utilize planned ignoring, the educator must investigate the function of the student's inappropriate behavior. If the function of the behavior is for access to attention, then planned ignoring may be appropriate. If the function of the behavior is for avoidance or escape, then it is not appropriate.

Before determining whether to use planned ignoring, the educator must look at the ramifications of the behavior. The behavior may become so disruptive to the other students that the teacher loses control of the entire group, then planned ignoring is not effective. Perhaps, the teacher has decided to ignore the student who is running around the room — the teacher needs to consider whether the student may then run out of the room or run out of the building and become a safety risk.

The educator must be consistent in the use of planned ignoring and decide whether he or she can "stick with the plan." If the educator has decided to ignore an inappropriate behavior and the student escalates the behavior, the educator may reach his/her breaking point and decide he or she cannot take it anymore. In the middle of the ignoring, the teacher breaks down and no longer ignores the behavior and issues a consequence. The student has learned a lesson — if he or she pushes the teacher so far the teacher will no longer ignore the behavior.

Planned ignoring must always be used with attention for the opposite appropriate behavior. If the student has his head down on the desk and is refusing to work and the teacher decides to ignore that behavior, then the teacher must reinforce the student when he is engaging in appropriate work behavior.

For younger students it is very effective to praise the student who is displaying appropriate behavior while utilizing planned ignoring for the student who is displaying inappropriate behavior. As an example, I like to visit kindergarten and first-grade classrooms, and invariably will find one or more students who are "off-task." I roam around the room and praise the students who are working, and those that are not quickly pick up on the fact that if they want my attention, they will need to be working. If teachers of younger students are waiting for students to pay attention before starting a lesson, they can comment: "I like the way Julie is paying attention." What generally will happen is that the other children will begin to pay attention so that they receive attention.

Planned ignoring is only appropriate for non-aggressive behaviors. It is not appropriate to ignore aggressive behavior because low-level aggression always turns into high-level aggression. Johns (2002) advises that behaviors that are disruptive, violate school rules, pose danger, or are aggressive in nature should never be ignored. Goldstein (1999) sees low-level aggression as the pathway to high-level aggression. As examples, he describes the authority conflict pathway that begins with stubborn behavior, moves to defiance, and culminates in authority avoidance. The covert behavior pathway starts with frequent lying, shoplifting, and moves on to property damage and culminates in moderate to serious covert delinquency, such as fraud or burglary. The overt behavior pathway commences with minor overt behaviors, such as annoying others or bullying, proceeds to individual or gang physical fighting, and then reaches the extremity of assault, rape, or other violent behavior. Minor acts of aggression turn into major acts of aggression.

Cautions in the Use of Planned Ignoring

1. Remember that the behavior will get worse before it gets better.

2. It is not appropriate to use planned ignoring if the function of the behavior is not for attention.

3. Planned ignoring is not appropriate for behavior that is so disruptive that other students cannot learn.

4. Planned ignoring is not appropriate for behavior that violates classroom and school rules; otherwise the student being ignored and the other students observe that the educator does not enforce the rules and condones violations of the rules.

5. Planned ignoring is not appropriate for behavior that could pose a danger to the student or to others. As an example, if a

student runs away from school and does not see the danger of going out into the street, the results could be deadly.

6. It is not appropriate to use planned ignoring for aggressive behavior. If the educator ignores aggressive behavior, he or she is sending a very bad message to the student that aggression is appropriate. Since the student will test the limits, the aggressive behavior will escalate. Low-level aggression will turn into high-level aggression.

References

Johns, B. (2002). *The paraprofessional's guide to managing student behavior: workbook.* Horsham, PA: LRP Publications.

Goldstein, A. (1999). *Low-level aggression: first steps on the ladder to violence.* Champaign, Illinois: Research Press.

Vaughn, S., Bos, C. and Schumm, J. (1997). *Teaching mainstreamed, diverse, and at-risk students in the general education classroom.* Boston: Allyn and Bacon.

Intervention #12 - Contracting

Scenarios

Let's look at this scenario below where contracting was very successful.

Contracting as a Successful Intervention Strategy

Mrs. Werder, a sixth-grade teacher, sits down and meets with Keasha and Keasha's mother because she is concerned about Keasha's lack of work completion. She is afraid that Keasha is going to fail her class. Mrs. Werder has made sure that Keasha is capable of completing the assignments that she is providing. She explains that she wants to help Keasha do better in school by completing her assignments. Mrs. Werder gets feedback from Keasha and her mom about what Keasha would like to earn if she did complete her assignments. Keasha explains that she likes to draw and would like some time in class to do her artwork. Together they determine that, for each assignment that Keasha completes, she can earn five minutes of time to do her artwork. They also determine that if Keasha completes all of her assignments for the day, she can have an additional 10 minutes at the end of the day to work on her art projects. Keasha's mother says that if Keasha completes all of her assignments for a given week, she will take Keasha to an art supply store and let her choose an item with a value of $10.00. Mrs. Werder types up the contract, and Keasha and her mother review it. They all agree to the terms of the contract and sign it. Mrs. Werder makes a copy for each of them, and Keasha posts her contract on her desk. This contract was a collaborative process, and Keasha, as well as her mother, had input. All parties accepted responsibility. The contract focused on positive behavior and also provided Keasha with an incentive that was meaningful to her.

Contrast the above example with this one.

Contracting as an Unsuccessful Intervention Strategy

Mr. Devine has decided to write a contract with a student in his high school social studies class. He meets with Larry, the student, and provides a list of six expectations for Larry and he outlines the consequences if he does not fulfill the terms of the contract. Larry refuses to sign the contract. What's wrong with this picture? Mr. Devine did meet with Larry, but did not provide any opportunity for Larry's input. He then listed six expectations for Larry, which was overwhelming to the student. Larry asked Mr. Devine what he would get if he did meet the expectations. Mr. Devine responded that he would not receive the consequences. There was no positive reinforcement for Larry.

Definition of Contracting

A contract can be defined as a written agreement by a student and the teacher or other staff member impacted by the student's behavior. The contract specifies the desired behavior of the student and the consequences, both positive and negative, of the behavior. The terms of the contract are mutually agreeable to the parties involved.

Sautner (2001) defined a student contract as a: "signed agreement regarding behavior, work habits, attendance, or other areas needing remediation, with strategies and ongoing evaluation included." (p. 214).

Vaughn, Bos and Schumm (1997) define a contract as either an oral or written agreement between a student and a teacher. The contract identifies the expected behavior and the consequences for exhibiting or not exhibiting that behavior.

Correct Use of Contracts

This author has found contracting to be most appropriate for students at the fifth-grade level or beyond; although some educators have reported it being successful for some younger students. When determining whether to use a contract, the educator must determine the targeted behavior and define that behavior. It is preferable to start with one behavior. Then the length of time that will determine whether the contract is met should be determined and, in the beginning, the duration should be a short one. The reward that the student will receive should be determined and should be such that it is reasonable for the expected behavior. The consequence of not engaging in the behavior is delineated. As an example, let's say that the teacher wants to increase the student's math homework assignments. The contract would delineate that the student will be expected to complete his/her math homework. To build in success, the teacher might start with completion of one night's homework. If the student completes the homework each night, he will receive 10 minutes of free time (the student likes to draw). It is important that the reward be something that is meaningful to the student. If the student does not complete the homework, he does not earn the free time and receives a "O" for his homework grade assignment. The contract also could include a reward for completing homework three days in a row. The student could receive a "homework pass" to get out of one homework assignment.

Zimmerman (2001) provides these guidelines: Contracts should be written in a collaborative process; they should be written in a positive manner, expectations should be clear, simple, and specific; assure input from others including the parents; tailor-make the contract for the specific student; all parties should have a signed copy of the contract; and the contract should be viewed as an enhancement; not a punishment.

Walker, Colvin and Ramsey (1995) have provided this checklist for setting up contracts:

1. Is the behavior selected something that the child is capable of doing?

2. Is the contract broken down into small steps?

3. Is there a time specified to check on the behavior each day?

4. Is there an incentive or list of incentives for the child?

5. Have I talked with the child and explained the expectations for both of us?

Cautions in the Use of Contracts

1. Contracts should first and foremost focus on the positive and not be punitive in nature. In Maine a 14-year-old with a learning disability was expelled from school for violating his contract. The contract utilized this language: "No swearing, no use of inappropriate words, no use of inappropriate sexual references. Quotations from published songs which contain offensive, threatening or otherwise inappropriate language may not be written or spoken in school, no written, verbal or

implied threatening of any person." Consequences included such things as warnings, being sent home, in-school or out-of-school suspension. There were no positive interventions in the contract. The hearing officer believed this was ineffective because it enumerated rules and punishments rather than establishing positive interventions. (*Westbrook Sch. Dep't (Me.)*, 32 IDELR 251 (2000).)

2. Contracts should not take the place of a behavioral intervention plan (BIP) in the IEP. Some school district personnel may build into the IEP the use of contracting and not provide any other behavioral interventions into the student's program. While contracting may be part of the BIP, it is not enough. The educators must address how replacement behaviors for the targeted areas will be addressed. If the student has a social skill deficit in a given area, how will that social skill be taught to the student. If the student is engaging in specific behaviors because of inappropriate academic tasks, how will those tasks be changed to address the needs of the student.

3. Contracts should be individualized for the student. At times, educators will develop contracts that are "one size fits all." Students who are exhibiting behavioral concerns that warrant the need for contracting need contracts that are tailor-made to meet their needs. Each student has specific target behaviors to increase and each student responds differently to certain incentives that may be built into the contract.

4. It is critical to monitor frequently the progress or lack of progress that the student is making. The educator needs to check on whether the contract is working with the student. Oftentimes, educators will do one of two things: Try the contract for a short period of time and determine it isn't working and just give up; or try the contract for a long period of time and find that it isn't working, but don't bother to investigate why it is not working. The use of contracting must be evaluated on a regular basis.

References

Sautner, B. (2001). Rethinking the effectiveness of suspension. *Reclaiming children and youth*, 9(4), 210-214.

Vaughn, S., Bos, C., and Schumm, J. (1997). *Teaching mainstreamed, diverse, and at-risk students in the general education classroom*. Boston: Allyn and Bacon.

Westbrook Sch. Dep't (Me.), 32 IDELR 251 (2000).

Zimmerman, B. (2001). *Why can't they just behave? a guide to managing student behavior disorders*. Horsham, PA: LRP Publications.

Walker, H., Colvin, G. and Ramsey, E. (1995). *Antisocial behavior in school: strategies and best practices*. Pacific Grove, Ca: Brooks/Cole.

103

Intervention #13 · One-on-One Paraprofessionals

The use of paraprofessionals in special education is growing. As schools find more students with significant needs, more one-on-one paraprofessionals are being employed. When students have behavioral challenges that require additional time for the teacher, paraprofessionals are being employed to help the student. In a study of parents' perceptions of paraprofessionals (Werts et al. 2004), 25 percent of the parents reported that paraprofessionals were there to keep the child focused, and 21 percent stated that the paraprofessionals were there because of behavioral issues. Fortunately in this study, most parents (75 percent) described the paraprofessional positively. We want the paraprofessional to help the student, not to hinder the student. We want the paraprofessional to promote independence, not reinforce learned helplessness or dependence. We want the paraprofessional to assist the student in giving a correct answer, not to give the child the answer.

Scenarios

Let's look at an example of a paraprofessional providing positive assistance to the student, then we will look at an example of a paraprofessional that may be doing more harm than good.

Paraprofessional Assistance Working

Jimmy is a fourth-grader who has difficulty staying on task. When he is off task he causes behavioral problems in the classroom. Those problems include out-of-seat behavior, making noises, and distracting other students from working by touching them and taking papers off of their desk. Jimmy is in a special education class for about one-half of his day and is in a general education fourth-grade class the remainder of the day. The IEP team has met, and it has been determined that Jimmy is in need of a one-on-one paraprofessional to assist his special education teacher and to accompany him into the general education classroom. The specific roles for the paraprofessional are delineated in the IEP and discussed during the preparation of the behavioral intervention plan. It is determined that the paraprofessional is needed in order to provide additional supervision for

Jimmy to make sure that he is not interrupting other students, also the paraprofessional will provide praise statements to Jimmy when he is working on task, and she will provide assistance to him when he has questions about the tasks he has been given by either teacher. The paraprofessional will provide a summary to each teacher on how Jimmy is doing in each setting.

Prior to her first day on the job, Mrs. Stallings (the paraprofessional) will participate in at least two days of positive behavior management training. Once on the job, the IEP team determines that the special education teacher, the general education teacher, and the paraprofessional, will meet weekly to discuss Jimmy's progress or lack thereof. The special education teacher and the general education teacher will pay particular attention to the amount of positive reinforcement that Mrs. Stallings is utilizing.

Now let's look at this scenario and figure out what is wrong with this picture.

Paraprofessional Assistance Not Working

Mrs. Johnson was employed last year to assist in the fifth-grade class as a paraprofessional. Mrs. Johnson has had three years of college training and meets the requirements of the No Child Left Behind Act. She grew up in the small community in which she is working and knows many of the families. She is also very active in a number of organizations within the community. Mrs. Johnson prides herself in being a "take charge" type of person. Last year she was assigned to work with Mrs. Hauter, a first-year teacher. She quickly let Mrs. Hauter know what she should and should not do. She also frequented the teacher's lounge where she talked about her frustration in working with Mrs. Hauter. Mrs. Johnson quickly became an expert in the school rules and reminded Mrs. Hauter when she observed that Mrs. Hauter had not followed the appropriate school procedures. At the end of the year, Mrs. Hauter asked that Mrs. Johnson not be reassigned to her. Since Mrs. Johnson is a very active and vocal member of the community, the superintendent and principal do not wish to release her. In August, a 9-year-old student with autism and challenging behavior moves into the district. The student's IEP indicates that the student was in a third-grade classroom and received resource special education programming, occupational and speech therapy. The IEP also shows that he had a one-on-one aide. The IEP team convenes to review the IEP and to determine their plan of action. The team recommends that the provisions of the previous IEP be followed. On the previous IEP there is no delineation of the specific role of the paraprofessional, and the current IEP team does not address the issue either.

The superintendent and principal determine that this will be the perfect solution for where to place Mrs. Johnson. The special education teacher and the third-grade teacher are busy preparing for the beginning of the school year and don't meet with Mrs. Johnson — after all Mrs. Johnson is experienced, well-known in the community and worked at the school last year. During the first week of school, Mrs. Johnson follows the child around and helps him with all of his assignments. When he runs from her, she chases after him and scolds him. When he won't do his work, she prods him along and, if he still does not complete the assignments, she reprimands him. When the student wants something, he points to the object and she gets it for him. She does not provide any positive reinforcement for him. Out in the community, she shares her everyday experiences with this child with other individuals in the organizations in which she belongs.

What is wrong with this picture? The IEP team failed to delineate the specific responsibilities for the paraprofessional. The paraprofessional received no special training prior to beginning her work with this child. The special education teacher and regular education teacher were not sure of the paraprofessional's role and did not establish how the paraprofessional would be supervised in her work. The paraprofessional also encouraged "learned helplessness" on the part of the student and did not provide positive reinforcement to the child when the child engaged in an appropriate activity. Utilizing her role in the community, Mrs. Johnson violated confidentiality laws when she spread the word about the child's daily actions.

Could this type of situation be found in other schools — the answer is a definite yes. Paraprofessionals may be actively involved in the community and know many of the families. They also may have difficulty understanding their roles and responsibilities in their position. It is up to school personnel to assure that such situations do not occur.

Definition of One-on-One Paraprofessional

The terms paraprofessionals and paraeducators can be used synonymously and defined as individuals who are employed to work alongside school professionals, providing instructional support and other related services to students under the supervision of school professionals. The terms refer to individuals whose job titles may be aide, instructional assistant, educational assistant, etc. (French 2004). Pickett is credited by French as the one to first use the title "paraeducator" to convey a level of training analogous to those outside the educational field such as paramedics and paralegals. One-on-one aides or paraprofessionals are those individuals who are hired for the specific purpose of providing assistance to one particular student. Again, that assistance is provided under the supervision of a certified teacher. In many instances, the student that the one-on-one aide is assigned to is a child with a significant disability.

The regulations accompanying the No Child Left Behind Act define a paraprofessional as an individual who provides instructional support. It does not include individuals who have only non-instructional duties such as providing support for computers, providing personal care services, or performing clerical duties. Educational responsibility should always be assigned to the teacher. The paraprofessional helps the teacher to accomplish his/her responsibility to deliver instruction.

The National Center on Educational Statistics (2000) reported a 48 percent increase in paraprofessionals between 1990-98. The National Resource Center for Paraprofessionals (2003) reported about 525,000 full-time paraprofessionals in 2001 — most serving students with disabilities in special education. According to the Study of Personnel Needs in Special Education (2001), the typical special education paraprofessional is a 44-year-old female who works in a regular elementary or secondary school. She has 6.5 years of experience in special education and 7.9 as a paraprofessional. Additional data from that study showed that paraprofessionals in special education have the following education:

High School diploma or less — 29%

Some college — 38%

Associate's degree or higher — 32%

Paraprofessional certificate or credential —13%

Teaching certificate or license — 6%

The addition of paraprofessionals to the field of special education is growing at a large rate. Assigning paraprofessionals to classrooms or individual students has become a growing and dominant model of support, especially for students with disabilities in inclusive classrooms, according to a report done be Giangreco and Broer (2003).

However neither research nor common sense provides the support for assigning the least trained personnel to provide primary instructional support for children with the most significant learning and behavioral challenges. Current work being done also suggests that the roles of paraprofessionals have steadily expanded to include teacher-type activities. Strengthening paraprofessional training was a focus of No Child Left Behind. That training is critical not only for paraprofessionals, but also for the teachers who provide supervision to the paraprofessional so that they gain a clear understanding of what their responsibilities are.

Correct Use of Paraprofessionals

We must assure the appropriate use of paraprofessionals when they are employed as a behavioral intervention support for a teacher who has direct responsibility for the education of a student with behavioral challenges. In order to do that, it is critical that the IEP team determine how the one-on-one aide will be utilized. The IEP team should determine for what specific purpose a paraprofessional is needed to assist in meeting the needs of the student with behavioral challenges. The team also should discuss what specific training is necessary for the paraprofessional and what is necessary for the teacher to be able to work with the paraprofessional. IDEA 2004 (as did IDEA 97) requires that support for school personnel be determined by the IEP. The IEP team must outline the following:

1. For what specific purpose is the one-on-one paraprofessional being employed?

a. Is the individual being employed to provide additional supervision of the student — another set of eyes and ears to watch the student?

b. Is the individual being employed to provide increased positive reinforcement to the student as a behavioral intervention?

c. Is the individual being employed to allow for inclusion of the student within a regular education classroom?

d. Is the individual needed to provide additional supervision for the student?

e. What parts of the behavioral intervention plan require the use of a one-on-one paraprofessional?

2. Who will provide the supervision of the paraprofessional, particularly if the student is assigned to an inclusive setting. The paraprofessional should be supervised by the special education teacher who has expertise in behavioral interventions. How will that supervision be provided? It is more difficult for the special education teacher to provide supervision within the general education classroom because she or he is not observing within that classroom all of the time. Therefore, communication between the special education teacher and the general education teacher will be critical to ensure needed supervision and support for the paraprofessional.

3. How will the individual student respond to an additional staff member assigned to him or her? For example, a student with autism may be bothered by another individual, particularly if the paraprofessional gets too close physically or guides the student by the hand when the student does not want to be touched.

4. How will the student's peers respond to him or her. In this author's experience, one must be very cautious in assigning a

one-on-one paraprofessional to a student who is in junior or senior high school. The adult assigned would call attention to the student before his peers and may embarrass and stigmatize him/her.

5. What type of monitoring system of the paraprofessional's role will take place? How often will the system be monitored? The IEP team has an obligation to monitor whether the work of the paraprofessional with the student is successful or not. If, after a reasonable time (usually not to exceed nine weeks), a team member observes that the paraprofessional is not assisting the student and may, in fact, be hindering progress, then that team member has an obligation to call a new IEP meeting.

6. What feedback system will be provided to the paraprofessional? Will daily meetings be held between the teacher and the paraprofessional? Will a behavior management specialist or other personnel meet with the teacher and paraprofessional on a regular basis?

7. The teacher should be involved in the interview process with the paraprofessional because it is critical that the teacher feel comfortable in working with that individual. It may be that the teacher does not have experience in providing supervision to a paraprofessional or that the teacher does not want another adult in his/her classroom. It may be that the personality type of the paraprofessional does not "click" with that of the teacher.

The minimal training content material for the individual paraprofessional should include:

1. The role of the paraprofessional.

2. Strategies for working with the supervisor.

3. Strategies for working with other school personnel.

4. An understanding of the specific needs of the individual student.

5. Issues surrounding confidentiality and ethics.

6. Positive behavioral interventions.

Cautions in the Use of One-on-One Paraprofessionals

1. Avoid assigning a paraprofessional to assist with a student with behavioral challenges until that paraprofessional has been provided specific training about positive behavioral interventions and understands the specific needs of the individual student.

2. Avoid employing an individual who has difficulty providing positive reinforcement to students. To work with any student with behavioral problems, adults must be able to accentuate the positive and provide praise to the student when the student is behaving appropriately. If the paraprofessional is providing attention to a student for negative behavior, that paraprofessional is going to do more harm than good.

3. Consider carefully the number of adults who are in the classroom to provide support to the teacher and the possible interactions among those individuals. This author is reminded of a special education teacher who, by October of the school year, was ready to quit because she had four one-on-one aides assigned to her classroom of six students and none of the one-on-one aides got along and frequently were getting into power struggles about who was supposed to do what. No teamwork was taking place and the students knew that and decided to play upon the weaknesses in the system.

4. Giangreco, Doyle, Halvorsen and Broer (2004) warn that excessive proximity of paraprofessionals is linked to detrimental effects such as dependence, interference with peer interactions, stigmatization, insular relationships, and actual provocation of behavior problems.

5. Giangreco and colleagues (2004) also warn that when individual paraprofessionals are employed for students with disabilities, there is a lower level of involvement of the teacher within an inclusive classroom. The teacher may feel less responsibility for the student because the paraprofessional is present. Likewise, the special educator who is supposed to be

providing the support to the paraprofessional may not be sufficiently involved with the paraprofessional within an inclusive setting — this is more likely to occur when the special educator has a large caseload and feels overburdened and, as a result, lets the paraprofessional make decisions alone.

Paraprofessionals can be an excellent support for a student with behavioral challenges. The key to their success is adequate training, direction, guidance, supervision, and feedback.

References

French, N. (2004). Introduction to the special series. *Remedial and Special Education*, 25(4), 203-204.

Giangreco, M., Doyle, M., Halvorsen, A., and Broer, S. (2004). Alternatives to over-reliance on paraprofessionals in inclusive schools. *Journal of Special Education Leadership*, 17(2), 82-90.

Giangreco, M. and Broer, S. (2003). The paraprofessional conundrum: why we need alternative support strategies. *TASH Connections*, 29(/3/4), 22-23.

National Center for Educational Statistics. (NCES) (2000). *Schools and staffing survey*. Washington, D.C: United States Department of Education. *nces.ed.gov/surveys/sass*.

Wallace, T. (2003). *Paraprofessionals: policies, practices and good ideas*. Minneapolis, MN: National Resource Center for Paraprofessionals. *nrcpara.org*.

United States Office of Special Education Programs. (2001). *Study of personnel needs in special education*. Washington, D. C: United States Department of Education. *www.spense.org*.

Werts, M., Harris, S., Tillery, C., and Roark, R. (2004). What parents tell us about paraeducators. *Remedial and Special Education*, 25(4), 232-239.

Intervention #14 – Written Reflection on Wrongful Behavior

Scenarios

Written Reflection Is an Appropriate Intervention

Spencer, a sixth-grader, has gotten into trouble on the school bus and he comes in to school very upset and is still yelling and swearing. The assistant principal takes Spencer to the timeout area where Spencer stands for five minutes until he is quiet. In the meantime, the principal talks with the bus driver to determine what happened on the bus. The bus driver asked Spencer to put up his window. Spencer refused to do so and started yelling obscenities at the driver. He then got out of his seat and went up to the front of the bus while the bus was moving and yelled at the driver. The driver pulled the bus over. The driver stayed very calm and explained to Spencer that he would not drive any farther until Spencer was in his seat and quiet. Spencer then returned to his seat and was quiet the rest of the way to school. During the preparation of Spencer's behavioral intervention plan on his IEP, it was determined that he frequently became agitated when he had to verbally explain an event in which he had gotten into trouble.

The IEP team had determined that a more preferred behavioral intervention for Spencer was to have him write down the specifics of the event. Spencer has a particular strength in written expression. The teacher developed a form for Spencer to use so that he could express himself in written reflection. After Spencer has been in the time-out room, the Assistant Principal takes Spencer to a separate room and provides him with the written reflection sheet. Spencer has to answer the following questions: What happened? What did you do? What could you do differently? Spencer is given a designated period of time to complete the sheet of paper. He also has to write a written apology to the bus driver. He will be required to give the apology to the driver that afternoon privately, but before he boards the bus to go home.

Now let's look at an inappropriate use of written reflection. (The following is a true story that involved this author some years ago.)

115

Written Reflection Is Not an Appropriate Intervention

The author was requested by a school to attend an IEP for a student who was having many behavioral problems. The student was swearing at school personnel, smoking cigarettes, skipping out of school after lunch, and exhibiting an array of other inappropriate behaviors that were of great concern in the school. The student was a young lady who was a ninth-grader. She was receiving services for students with learning disabilities and had an identified deficit in the area of written expression. The young lady was present, along with her mother, and another woman who identified herself as an "advocate." We were in the process of developing the BIP and discussing appropriate interventions. The "advocate" spoke up and suggested this wonderful intervention that she had seen used in another school called: "written reflection." After an inappropriate behavior was exhibited, the student had to complete a form that asked these questions: Why did you engage in the behavior? and What could you have done differently? The advocate thought this was a wonderful idea. This author obviously was shocked that this individual had not recognized that this was an inappropriate intervention for a student with a learning disability in written expression. The author pointed out to the "advocate" that such an intervention might indeed cause even more behavioral problems. One also would question the value of having a student write down why they did what they did — because many times that gives the student the perfect opportunity to blame someone else for the problem and to not accept responsibility for his/her own behavior.

Definition of Written Reflection on Wrongful Behavior

This process is used as a consequence when a student has engaged in inappropriate behavior and school personnel want the student to spend time analyzing, in writing, what he or she did wrong and other appropriate alternatives to the inappropriate behavior. Some schools actually have a pre-determined form that is utilized during in-school suspension. The student is given a pre-printed worksheet and asked to answer specific questions about the inappropriate behavior in which the student engaged, or the teacher may give the student a blank sheet of paper and have the student write what the student did and what they could do differently the next time a similar situation occurs other than engage in the inappropriate behavior that got he or she into trouble.

Correct Use of Written Reflection

Reflection can be a very effective teaching tool. We have all learned from our mistakes, especially when we take the responsibility of reflecting on specific events that have been problematic for us. We can then realize that we had the choice of acting differently within the situation. We also can analyze the situation after the fact and learn from that analysis. This is the premise upon which reflection is based — thinking about what happened and what could have been done differently to prevent a similar negative occurrence in the future.

The most helpful questions for reflection include: What happened? — the student is expected to reflect on the details of the event that got the student into trouble; What did you do? — the student focuses on what he/she actually did and does not focus on blaming someone else; and, What could you do the next time this happens? — the student focuses on the future and what options or alternatives there are to choose from the next time he or she is in a similar situation.

At times written reflection can calm down a student, rather than verbally reflecting on the situation. Students may become agitated when they verbally talk about an event, but when they are writing down the events, they may become thoughtful and quiet while taking the time to reflect.

Teaching a student the process of reflection is a lifelong self-management technique. The student learns that he or she may want to keep a journal for recording events that happen in his/her everyday life that may be upsetting.

Cautions in the Use of Written Reflection

1. This practice is not appropriate for students with significant written expression or fine motor problems. Written reflection will cause the student increased frustration when he or she is already angry anyway because the student knows that he or she will have difficulty with the task. As an alternative, it may be better for the teacher to talk with the student

117

about the event rather than having him/her write about it. Another option is for the student to record his/her answers into a tape recorder and to listen to the recording.

2. Questions such as "Why did you do what you did?" should be avoided. Reflection should focus on the behavior exhibited in the incident, what the student could have done differently, and what the student can do the next time that a similar situation arises. Focusing on the specifics of an event causes a student to actually look at the specific behavior he/she exhibited and what he/she could have done differently.

Written reflection can be a very effective behavioral intervention if based on the specific skills and needs of the student.

Intervention #15 – Use of Computers as a Behavioral Intervention

Scenarios

Imagine this fifth-grade classroom situation where computer technology as a behavioral intervention is used effectively.

Effective Use of a Computer as an Intervention Tool

Lonnie has had significant behavioral challenges in the past and Mrs. Bean, the teacher, knows that she will need to provide motivating strategies for Lonnie. She introduces the use of e-mail dialogue journals with her students. At the beginning of each day, she requests that her students send her an e-mail about their previous day's activities and share with her any questions or concerns they have. She then responds to those e-mails at the end of the day. Each morning when the students come in, they can read her personal e-mail to them and respond. In her e-mails, she makes positive statements to the students about their progress from the previous day. Lonnie really enjoys this personal message from Mrs. Bean. Mrs. Bean also has her students write an individual goal for the day. At the end of the day, the students reflect on whether they met their goal. She gives the students the choice of charting their progress on a graph utilizing the computer. Lonnie really enjoys doing this. Mrs. Bean knows that writing assignments can be difficult for Lonnie so she gives him the choice of either using paper and pencil or the computer so he can have the benefit of spell check and other needed tools. Lonnie always chooses to use the computer because the written assignments seem to be easier for him when he can type the information. Lastly, math is not Lonnie's favorite subject so Mrs. Bean allows Lonnie to use the computer for five minutes for a math game if he has worked on his math assignment for 15 minutes. Lonnie finds that math can be fun.

In this example, Mrs. Bean used technology in several ways as an effective behavioral intervention tool. She used e-mail as a way to provide positive comments and support to her students. She also used a choice activity for writing for Lonnie — he could write using paper and pencil, or he could use the computer. She also allowed him to graph his progress on his daily goal. Lastly she utilized the Premack

Principle (see pg. 17) — if Lonnie completed so much of his work, he would be allowed to use the computer for a math game.

Now let's look at this example of how Mrs. McGray inappropriately offered the computer as an intervention tool in her classroom.

Inappropriate Use of a Computer as an Intervention Tool

Mrs. McGray, an eight-grade English teacher, is scheduled to have Jeremy, a student with autism, in her classroom for fifth period. She is very nervous about having a child with autism as her student. She has been told that Jeremy likes computers. Mrs. McGray is working on how to write reports with her students, and Jeremy starts acting up because he doesn't want to write a report. Mrs. McGray tells Jeremy to go over and work on the computer. Jeremy does and decides to play a game on the computer. Mrs. McGray is relieved that Jeremy is quiet so she allows him to stay on the computer for the rest of the period. The next day, Jeremy, again, does not want to work on his report and starts acting up. Mrs. McGray, again, allows him to work on the computer. Mrs. McGray is very pleased that she has figured out how to keep Jeremy from throwing a tantrum. How much educational benefit is Jeremy receiving? Jeremy has indeed manipulated the teacher — he doesn't want to write and has learned that if he throws a tantrum, he will not have to engage in the writing activity.

The increased availability and use of computer technology within the school setting has brought a whole new wave of challenges to school personnel — how to utilize the computer to enhance instruction, how to use the computer for reinforcement of specific skills, and how to supervise the use of computers within the classroom. This section will focus on the use of computers as a behavioral intervention tool. Computers have enormous positive potential for students with emotional/behavioral disorders and can make learning motivating for students who may be the most difficult to motivate.

Definition of the Use of Computers for Behavioral Interventions

Computers for instruction can be defined as tools for enhancing instruction and reinforcement of instruction by the teacher. The purpose of computers is to significantly enhance learning within the classroom. Technology in the form of computers should be used to support learning objectives. The utilization of computers for instruction can be very motivating to students with emotional/behavioral disorders because of the quick speed and immediate feedback that can be provided to the student.

Universal design principles offer a wealth of opportunities for students with special needs. In universal design, print materials are digitized so that multiple accommodations can be made: highlighting the text word by word, reading aloud the material as the student follows on the screen, additional descriptions of the material, and immediate feedback on answers. There are an increasing number of textbook publishers that are making electronic text versions of their books available so that the books can be altered as an accommodation (Johns and Crowley 2003).

Computers also can be utilized to create products such as presentations or reports or graphs of student progress. For behavioral purposes, a student might be able to chart his/her own progress on behavioral goals or chart his/her academic progress so the student can visually see how much success has been achieved. Since choices are a very effective behavioral intervention tool, the teacher can provide a choice on how to create a product about a studied topic. The student might make a Powerpoint presentation or an Excel spreadsheet.

Computers with Internet access also can be utilized for research on a specific topic and for communication with other students or with the teacher. Teachers can communicate with students via e-mail. Some teachers have good success with dialogue journals where students write notes about activities and then the teacher writes back to the student — this is an excellent communication strategy — and e-mail lends itself well to the dialogue journal process.

Computers also can be used as an effective positive reinforcement strategy. If the student completes a given number of written assignments, the student might be able to work on a specified activity on the computer — this is known as the Premack Principle (see pg. 17). The student completes a non-preferred task and then gets to work for a given period of time on a preferred task — in this case, the computer.

Correct Use of Computers

Armstrong (1999) points out that computer technology is a highly effective approach for students identified as having ADD/ADHD. Advantages include instant feedback that is high speed, bright colors, sounds, interaction. He also points out that we can bore children with some software programs; as an example, electronic versions of worksheets or textbooks that were not of interest to the children in the first place. Judicious use of high stimulation technology can provide an excellent resource to help students acquire information in a manner that coordinates with their "hyper-minds" (Armstrong, p. 67).

Technology also may be used effectively as a self-management tool for students to chart their data on their behavioral or academic improvement. As an example, the teacher and student are working together to reduce the number of talk-outs of the student. Each time the student talks out, he has to make a check mark on a piece of paper. He can then graph the reduction of talk outs. Perhaps the teacher and student are working on word recognition skills. Each time the student masters a word, he can add that word to his chart — the student could make his or her own spreadsheet.

Technology also can be utilized as an alternative to worksheets. Rather than practicing skills using a worksheet, the student can do a Powerpoint presentation. Instead of writing spelling words, the student can use a word processing program. With technology there is a wealth of choice options for assignments.

Hawkes and Cambre (2001) studied the impact of the increased use of technology by conducting interviews with teachers and other education leaders. Some behavioral outcomes were: increased attendance, excitement and interest in learning, more engaged problem solving, increased acceptance of responsibility, increase in depth and extent of conversations with teachers and other students, improved style of presentations by students, and increased self-esteem.

Universal design offers a whole array of opportunities for accommodating student needs.

Technology can be utilized as a way to engage an otherwise disenfranchised student. The student may be resistant to reading, especially in front of other students. Technology can be a motivating tool for the student to read.

A new twist is being used to provide teacher instruction in appropriate classroom behavior. d'Oliveira (2004) reviewed a program known as PEGS — Practice in Effective Guidance Strategies. The program is a game style and computer based. It is designed to help teachers improve their behavior management techniques. The program is now available to every elementary school teacher in Georgia. The program consists of hypothetical scenarios of classrooms with students whose behaviors range from full participation to disruption. Within the program, the teacher picks a student behavior and chooses a particular response to that behavior. If the selection is a positive one, the hypothetical classroom of students begins to participate in a lesson. If it is the wrong strategy, problem behaviors increase. Preschool and secondary versions have been written for preschool and secondary schools with a grant from the Office of Special Education Programs (d'Oliveira 2004).

Cautions in the Use of Computers in Instruction

1. Programs that promote violence should not be used within the school setting. There are a number of computer games that depict violence. Some send inappropriate messages to students. Some computer games show violence where the characters die and then when the student turns the computer off and back on the characters reappear.

2. Staff should continuously monitor students. Currently there are too many opportunities for students who are utilizing the computer to access inappropriate Web sites before the teacher knows what happened. The computer also provides an opportunity for some students to send threatening or harassing e-mails.

3. Schools must have clear policies and procedures on the use of computers. Such policies must address appropriate use and consequences for inappropriate use. It is also advisable to have staff and students sign an agreement to abide by the policies that govern the use of the computer.

4. The computer should not be used as a substitute for teacher instruction. Students need teacher time to be taught, review,

reinforce skills, and gain social interaction and establish a rapport with the student.

5. Computers should not be sitting in the room only to be used after schoolwork is completed. "If we are to realize technology's potential to transform teaching and learning, it must plan an integral role, not peripheral role, in classrooms. It must be part of the schoolwork, not something to do after the schoolwork is done" (Eib 2001, p. 23).

6. Avoid overuse of the computer and never use it as a substitute for instruction or social skills training. If the student is allowed to work alone at the computer all day, he or she is failing to learn social skills needed to get along with classmates and other people in the everyday world that the student will encounter. An alternative to this as recommended by Eib suggests that pairs of students and small groups can support one another's learning and optimize the use of technology as a collaborative learning tool.

7. It is appropriate to use the computer as a reinforcement for positive behavior or completion of work, but the software that is the reinforcement should be relevant to the educational goals of the classroom. This author has witnessed teachers allowing students to use software games that are not related to instruction, or even worse, software games that promote aggression and violence.

In this day and age of advanced technology, there are multiple opportunities for appropriate behavioral interventions utilizing computers.

References

Armstrong, T. (1999). *ADD/ADHD alternatives in the classroom.* Alexandria, VA: Association for Supervision and Curriculum Development.

d'Oliveira, S. (Editor) (2004). Software aims to curb class behavior problems. *The school discipline advisor.* 6(7), 2.

Eib, B. J. (2001). Evaluating technology use in the classroom. *Principal leadership*. 1(9), 16-23.

Hawkes, M. and Cambre, M. (2001). Educational technology. Identifying the effects. *Principal Leadership*. 1(9), 48-51.

Johns, B. and Crowley, E. (2003). *Students with disabilities and general education*. Horsham, PA: LRP Publications.

Intervention # 16 - Proximity Control

Scenarios

The process of moving physically closer to the student can be an effective behavioral intervention tool. Let's look at this example of how Mr. Warner utilizes the technique correctly in his classroom.

Proximity Control Used Effectively

Mr. Warner teaches high school social studies and incorporates many project-based assignments in his classroom. He may lecture for a period of time on a topic and then provide choices for students to show what they have learned about the material. He also assigns students to work in small groups to review their notes on the lectures. Mr. Warner has three students in his class who have been diagnosed with ADHD but spend the majority of their school day in general education classes. He also has a student — Alec — in his class who spends the majority of the day in an instructional classroom for students with emotional/behavioral disabilities. When Mr. Warner is lecturing, he utilizes Powerpoint with a remote control so he can move around the room as he lectures. For Alec and the three students with ADHD, he provides a copy of his Powerpoint notes. As he lectures and comes to specific vocabulary words, he moves to Alec's desk and points to the words. He also gives Alec a nod when he is paying attention. For the three students who have ADHD, he strives to move by them when he is coming to a concept that he believes might be difficult for them. He smiles at them when they are paying attention and gives them a positive sign as he moves by them. When it is time for the students to get into groups and compare their notes, he makes sure that he moves toward the groups in which Alec and the three students with ADHD are participating. When Mr. Warner is explaining an individual assignment, he makes sure that he moves to where Alec is working as well as the other three students with ADHD to check to see if they understand the assignment. Mr. Warner also moves around the room during the time students are working on individual assignments in order to assist any student who is having difficulty.

Mr. Warner's constant movement around the room utilizes proximity control as an effective behavioral intervention. He prevents many problems because, while he is moving, he is observing his students carefully and looking for any signs of frustration so that he can assist the student. He is also providing heightened supervision for his students. He knows what is going on because he is watching as he moves around the room. He is cueing students positively by pointing to keywords in directions and new vocabulary words. He is also providing praise for appropriate behavior, and he provides support for his students by being close to them when they need him for a question or a problem with any of their work. By his proximity, he provides reassurance to his students.

Now let's see what is wrong with this picture in the same school building in another classroom.

Proximity Control Used Incorrectly

Down the hall, Mrs. Jones teaches a basic English class where she has the three students who have ADHD. Mrs. Jones believes she is using proximity control, but it is not working in her classroom. The students with ADHD are misbehaving, and she doesn't understand why. Mrs. Jones utilizes lecture followed by independent writing activities. When she is lecturing and one of the students starts misbehaving, she moves closer to that student and corrects him loud enough that the other students can hear. When Mrs. Jones provides a written assignment to her students, she moves to each of the students with ADHD. She repeats the assignment she has given to the whole group and stands over them until they start the assignment. She finds that one of the students does not start the assignment so she continues to stand over him, and he then refuses to start the assignment.

What did Mrs. Jones do wrong? She utilized proximity control paired with criticism of the student. She only moved over to the students when they misbehaved. Therefore she was giving her attention only for negative, rather than positive, behavior. Mrs. Jones did go over to the students to clarify her directions, but, after doing so, she did not know when to move away from them to give them some space. If she would have moved away from the students after utilizing proximity control, she would have increased her chances that the intervention was effective. Read on for more details.

Definition of Proximity Control

Jordan (1999) noted that proximity control can be defined as the educator standing closer to the child than he or she was when the child is beginning to have a problem with behavior. Less effective is for the child to move closer to the teacher. Proximity should not be seen as a threat to the child, but rather as a respectful behavior management tool. It is most effective when used during question and answer periods or when giving directions, or it can be paired with preventive cueing for some students. Preventive cueing is when the teacher moves closer to the student and gives a recognized signal that the teacher has taught to the student, such as a hand movement to lower the voice or to remember to raise his/her hand.

Correct Use of Proximity Control

Proximity control can be a very effective behavioral intervention and can result in a significant decrease in behavioral problems within a classroom. This author is reminded of a first-year teacher who was working with adolescents with significant behavioral problems and was doing an excellent job in meeting the academic and behavioral needs of her students. When asked to what she attributed her success, she stated: "proximity control." She commented that she made a point of moving around the room working constantly with her students during instruction and during independent activities.

Proximity control can be a very effective prevention tool. When an educator is close to a student he may be able to pick up subtle warning signals that the student is becoming frustrated. By standing near the student who is frustrated or starting to argue about a situation, an educator can often diffuse the situation.

Proximity control can be utilized to provide closer supervision of a student whose mind may wander during a question and answer period or when a teacher is giving directions, or to closely supervise a student who may engage in inappropriate behaviors when the student thinks that the teacher is not watching. There is an increasing population of students that require more supervision entering schools today than there had been in the past. Students may engage in inappropriate behaviors such as touching other students, mumbling under their breaths, stealing, and cheating. When a teacher is administering a test,

129

it is a good idea to move around the room to watch students closely to see whether their eyes are on their own papers.

Proximity control also can be a valuable tool in providing reassurance to a student who may find an activity to be difficult. At times a student may need to have someone beside him so that he knows if he has a problem there is a helping hand standing by.

Proximity control can be used as a tool to provide an additional visual cue for a student who has difficulty following verbal directions only. As an example, if the teacher has given a student an assignment from a workbook, he or she should always review key vocabulary words on the assignment and key directions for the students. If the teacher is giving the assignment to an entire group, he or she can stand by a particular student and point to the key vocabulary words in the assignment and also point to the directions that the assignment provides. The teacher also can develop a behavioral cue for a student — a visual signal to begin a task or to calm down.

Proximity control can be a valuable positive reinforcement tool. For younger students who need visual and verbal positive feedback, the teacher can move around the room making positive statements and/or provide a tangible token or a point for appropriate behavior. For older students, the teacher might make a positive statement to a student quietly or give the student a personal handwritten note of praise. Remember that some older students may not want to be reinforced in front of their peers so proximity control can be an excellent way of giving praise privately to the student.

Proximity control should be used as a way to engage in respectful behavior management. If a student who sits in the back of the room is acting up, it would be disrespectful to correct that student from the front of the room. Doing so calls attention to the negative behavior in front of the student's peers. This is embarrassing to the student and will build resentment. It is much more appropriate for the teacher to move to the area where the student is sitting so that the teacher can prevent a behavioral problem from occurring in the first place. Mendler (1992) referred to the P.E.P. method for communicating expectations for students to correct their behavior: Privacy, Eye Contact, and Proximity. He cautions that when using eye contact, the educator must be sensitive to cultural or emotional issues.

Cautions in the Use of Proximity Control

1. Proximity control should not be utilized as a controlling tool when a student becomes aggressive. As a matter of fact, it is important that the educator refrain from "invading a student's space" when that student is angry. A rule of thumb for how close to stand to an angry student is at least 1 and ½ to 3 feet away from the student (Johns and Carr 1997). That distance gives the student the space that he or she needs to calm down. Staff also should remember that they should stand at an angle from that distance. If they stand eyeball to eyeball and face to face, the stance is perceived as confrontational by the student and will escalate the aggression.

2. The author's favorite behavior management saying is: **"Be positive, be brief, and be gone."** The importance of positive reinforcement has been repeated throughout this book. When giving a direction to a student, the educator should frame the direction in **positive** terms. When giving a direction to a student, the educator should use the minimum number of words possible — **be brief**. The student may have a problem with processing information given verbally, therefore the less number of words in the direction the better. The student also may have an auditory memory deficit, meaning that the student has difficulty remembering what he or she hears. If the educator gives a long and involved direction, the student may not be able to execute the direction because he or she simply does not remember what it was. And, when an educator has given a direction to the student, the educator should refrain from standing over him or her watching to see if the student is going to complete the task. The teacher should leave — or, more simply put, **be gone**. Students may need space, and, more importantly, they may need to "save face." If the educator is standing over the student, the student may perceive the action as confrontational and "dig in his heels" and refuse to complete the direction. Here is a true life example involving this author when she was a school administrator. One day a young lady (Alice) had a confrontation with her boyfriend in the same classroom. Alice was very angry and became boisterous and was brought out of the classroom by her teacher who

131

then called for my assistance. We were able to calm down Alice using a calm approach and give her alternatives to deal with the situation. It was then time for Alice to return to the classroom, but she refused. The teacher very calmly gave her the direction: "Alice, I need you to come back in the classroom now. I know you can have a good rest of the day." The teacher then went back into the classroom, and I started to move away from Alice toward my office. Alice then re-entered the classroom within a few seconds. We allowed Alice the opportunity to "save face" and gave her some additional time to make her own decision. If we would have continued to stand with Alice and watched her every move, she most likely would not have gone back into the classroom. This was a time when proximity control would not have worked.

3. Be very cautious in utilizing proximity control where the student must come to the teacher, rather than the preferred method of moving to the student. The teacher should be actively engaged with his/her students and should be moving toward them; it is less disruptive for the student if utilized in this manner. At times, the teacher will want to sit at his/her own desk and have the student come up with questions. Several problems can arise as a result of this technique. The student may get into trouble on his way to the desk. The student may forget to bring the assignment or a writing utensil with him/her to the desk. While the teacher is sitting at his or her desk, it is difficult to attend to the other students in the class and those students may begin to have problems or engage in inappropriate activities.

Proximity control can be an effective preventive and intervention tool for positively changing behavior. Its correct uses and benefits are many. This section has provided you with some ways to implement this intervention effectively.

References

Johns, B. and Carr, V. (1997). *Techniques for managing verbally and physically aggressive students*. Second edition. Denver: Love Publishing.

Jordan, D. (1999). *Positive behavioral interventions: parents need to know.* Minneapolis, Minnesota: PACER Center.

Mendler, A. (1992). *What do I do when . . .? How to achieve discipline with dignity in the classroom.* Bloomington, Indiana: National Educational Service.

Intervention # 17 - Antiseptic Bouncing

Think of a difficult task with which you are faced. You are working at the task and become frustrated, you decide to move away from the task for a short period of time to get a glass of water or a cup of coffee, you return to the task and feel better about continuing your work. You are engaging in antiseptic bouncing. You have learned to take a break and change activities for a short period of time when you are frustrated.

Let's look at this example of how antiseptic bouncing is used effectively as a behavioral intervention in Mrs. Steinberg's classroom.

Scenarios

Antiseptic Bouncing Used Effectively

Mrs. Steinberg is a seventh-grade math teacher. One of her students, Craig, in her fifth-period class, becomes easily frustrated when doing his math assignments. She has worked to decrease the amount of independent work that she gives Craig to do at one time. She also has learned to see the signs that Craig is getting frustrated in his work. He sometimes gets the "death grip" on his pencil and starts frowning and making increased erasures. She has learned that when she sees this frustration, she needs to utilize "antiseptic bouncing." She writes an innocuous note to the office to the school secretary. The note might state how many students in her class are staying after school or what activity she is currently working on in her class or provide a list of supplies that she needs. She moves over to Craig and asks him if he will take the note to the office for her and then return right away. She has discussed this with the school secretary and the school principal and they are in agreement that when they see Craig coming into the office with the note they simply will smile, take the note, and tell Craig to have a great rest of the day. That short break makes a world of difference in Craig's outlook. When he returns to class, Mrs. Steinberg thanks him. When he returns to his desk, she moves over to him and asks if she can assist him in the assignment. She also has used this technique effectively with Joe, who is in her last period math class. When she observes that Joe is becoming frustrated, she makes a request that he collect the chalk on the chalkboard for her. This task

135

takes him about two minutes. He then returns to his seat, and Mrs. Steinberg thanks him and asks if she can assist him in completing the assignment.

Let's now look at antiseptic bouncing used incorrectly in Mrs. Simmons' classroom.

Antiseptic Bouncing Used Incorrectly

Mrs. Simmons teaches a sixth-grade classroom of 24 students. Bill is in her classroom, and Bill makes it clear from the beginning of the year that he does not like to do social studies. When it is time for a social studies independent task, Bill will begin to disrupt the classroom by talking to his neighbors or by getting up to sharpen his pencil and tapping on other students' desks on the way to the sharpener. Mrs. Simmons decides she will utilize antiseptic bouncing, and, when Bill is being disruptive, she sends him to the office with a note that states to the secretary and principal that Bill is being disruptive. On the way to the office, Bill stops and gets a drink of water, talks with anyone in the hall, and "hangs out in the hall" for about 10 minutes. When he finally arrives in the office, the principal reads the note, reprimands Bill and sends him back to class. Bill stops in the restroom, gets a drink, and then returns to class about 10 minutes later. By the time Bill returns to class, the time for independent work in social studies is over and Bill will have to take the work home with him since he did not get it done in class.

What went wrong here with "antiseptic bouncing"? Mrs. Simmons is actually sending Bill to the office for what she sees as punishment; yet, she is reinforcing Bill for his inappropriate behavior. Bill has manipulated the situation. He doesn't want to do social studies, and he has learned that if he becomes disruptive in class, Mrs. Simmons will send him to the office. He then can waste instructional time in the hall and restroom. When he gets to the office, he is reprimanded for his behavior, but this doesn't bother him because he is getting out of the activity that he didn't want to do in the first place.

Definition of Antiseptic Bouncing

Antiseptic bouncing can be defined as a short-time removal or break for a student from an activity that may be difficult. Beck, Coleman and Wineman (1985) used the term to describe what can be a very effective behavioral intervention. In antiseptic bouncing, the teacher gives the student a chore, such as delivering a note to the secretary or principal in the office, to allow the student a short break from the task at hand (Johns and Carr 1997). The change in an activity can be sufficient to drain off a student's frustration so that the student can begin again after returning from the break.

Correct Use of Antiseptic Bouncing

Antiseptic bouncing should be used when the educator observes early warning signs that a student is becoming frustrated with a task. The educator needs to know the student's triggers for frustration — specific activities that the student may perceive as too difficult, an upsetting comment by a peer, or an earlier occurrence on the bus. Antiseptic bouncing should be used after the teacher has tried supportive assistance and active listening to find out what is specifically causing the student to have problems with a particular task. But at times, supportive assistance and active listening may not be effective with the student and the student needs to be able to "take five" — take a short break away from a task so that he or she can return after a short period of time and face the challenge. Antiseptic bouncing should not be used when an educator believes that the student may be manipulating the situation in order to completely avoid a task. It should be used for a very short period of time — a break of no more than five minutes generally is most effective. The educator must carefully plan for its use — where the student will be able to go to take a break or run an errand. Can an errand or a chore be done within the classroom without being disruptive to the other classmates? If not, are personnel in the school office willing to participate in the behavioral intervention. If they are willing to participate, is the office close enough that the teacher can see the student travel to the office? If not, is there another adult within the classroom who can accompany the student? If not, is it safe to send the student to the office alone?

Cautions in the Use of Antiseptic Bouncing

1. Utilize antiseptic bouncing as a short-term break for a student. Generally no more than five minutes away from a task can give a student an opportunity to regroup and face the challenging activity that awaits him. If the break time is too long, you are allowing the loss of significant academic time. At times, a break to go and sharpen a pencil or get a drink of water may be sufficient time for the student to regroup.

2. Be very cautious that you are not allowing the student to manipulate a situation in order to avoid doing the task completely. At times a student may want to take a break away from an activity and while doing so will continue to engage in avoidance behaviors — as a result the student will be away from the task too long. As an example, a student might be given a note to take to the office, but while in the office the student visits with the secretary and the principal, and generally hangs around the office and fails to return to class within the prescribed period of time. To avoid such an occurrence, it is a good idea to give the student a very specific time deadline for when he or she must return. For those students who do not have a sense of time, the teacher may want to use a specific timer or write the time on the board by which the student is to return. When the student returns within the prescribed amount of time, he or she should then be verbally reinforced for returning and for running the errand, and then the teacher should start to assist the student in getting started again with the task.

3. The educator also will need to educate those who are involved in using this behavioral intervention. As an example, if the teacher is going to have the student run an errand to the office, it should be discussed ahead of time with the school secretary and the school principal to see whether they are willing to have the student come to the office. It is most beneficial if the secretary and/or school principal also will verbally reinforce the student when the student gets to the office. In the real world of schools, we all know that there are many

times when the office is very busy, so the educator will want to avoid sending the student during those times.

4. The educator also will need to provide some sort of supervision of the student when the student runs the errand. If the educator has the luxury of having an assistant, perhaps the assistant can accompany the student. If the educator does not have another individual to assist, then he or she must judge whether it is safe to allow the student to go to the office or whether it would be better to give the student another chore or errand to do that does not require him/her to be out of the teacher's sight. He could be directed to sharpen pencils, or to go to the office while the teacher stands in the hallway.

By utilizing antiseptic bouncing, you are teaching the student a lifetime skill that he or she can use when faced with difficult tasks.

References

Beck, M., Coleman, T., and Wineman, D. (1985). *Managing the unmanageable student.* Lexington, MA: Ginn Press.

Johns, B. and Carr, V. (1997). *Techniques for managing verbally and physically aggressive students.* Second edition. Denver: Love Publishing.

Intervention #18 - Self-Management Techniques — Goal-Setting and Self-Monitoring of Rules

All educators must avoid techniques that generate "learned helplessness" on the part of their students. Our ultimate goal should be to teach our students how to monitor their own behavior. Self-management techniques strive to do just that, if used correctly. Gears are switched; instead of the educator monitoring and controlling the student's behavior, the student monitors his/her own behavior — an excellent life skill that promotes independence for the life that awaits the student when he leaves the school setting.

Let's look at how Mrs. Wilson used two self-management techniques within her classroom.

Scenarios

Effectively Using Self-Management Techniques

Mrs. Wilson is a fourth-grade teacher in a school where the philosophy is one of positive interventions. She utilizes a high degree of positive reinforcement within her classroom and believes that at the fourth-grade level her students should learn to manage their own behavior. Each morning when her students arrive, she spends the first 10 minutes talking about the importance of establishing a goal for what each of the students wants to accomplish for the day. Along with the students, she provides an overview of the day and talks about what <u>her</u> goal for the day is. As an example, she shares with the students in her class that her goal for that one day is to make a positive statement to each one of them. Another day she says her goal is to individually assist each student for at least five minutes. She then talks with the students about what they might establish for a goal for themselves that day. The students brainstorm ideas, and she reinforces them for original and positive ideas. She then gives each student a goal sheet. The goal sheet looks like this:

141

Student's Name_____

Today is_____

My goal for today is:_____

Did I meet my goal?	Before lunch	Yes/No
	After lunch	Yes/No

Prior to lunch, Mrs. Wilson spends a few minutes reviewing with her students whether she is making progress toward her goal. She then has the students spend time looking at their individual goals and answering on the sheet whether they believe they are making progress toward their goal. If they don't believe they are making progress, she stresses that they still have the afternoon to work on it. At the end of the day, she once again reviews her goal and provides the students a chance to individually review their goals. She then moves around the room to see how students have done. If students wish to share their successes of the day with the class, they can do so and the teacher positively reinforces the student for that. If students do not reach their goals, she encourages them to quietly reflect on what they could have done differently that day.

At the beginning of the year, Mrs. Wilson also worked with her students to establish the rules of the classroom. The rules that she and the students came up with were as follows:

Raise your hand and wait for the teacher to call on you; stay in your seat unless you have permission to move; keep your hands and feet to yourself; and respect the school's and each other's property.

The rules are posted in the classroom and each morning the teacher reviews them with the students. There is also a pictorial depiction of each rule and an actual picture of a student following the rule. Each student is given a copy of the rules. At the end of every 30-minute period of time, the teacher has the student put a check mark next to the rules that he/she has followed. She then moves around the classroom providing individual feedback to each student and reinforcing those who have followed the rules. If she notices that a student has checked that he or she followed a specific rule, and she does not believe that this was an accurate assessment, she will talk with the student privately about his/her assessment. However she has found that the students are stricter in their assessment of their own behavior than she would be. By the end of the first quarter, she remakes the sheets and has the students monitor on an hourly basis. By the end of the first semester, the students are monitoring their own behavior every two hours. By the end of the year, she is pleased that this activity can be done only once at the end of the day when the students also review their own goals.

Now let's look at another classroom in the building.

Ineffectively Using Self-Management Techniques

Mrs. Spencer has heard Mrs. Wilson talk about her success with goal setting and the students' self-monitoring of rules. Mrs. Spencer decides to try a similar approach. She provides a sheet of paper similar to the one that Mrs. Wilson used. The students write their goal for the day, but Mrs. Spencer decides that she does not have time to monitor the goals in the morning and will wait until the end of the day to spend time with the students monitoring their goals. She sees no need to write her own goal for the day. At the end of the day things usually get busy, and she doesn't always have the time to spend with the students monitoring their goals, so she waits until the next day. She decides that on those days she will just have the students continue their goals from the day before and do the monitoring at the end of that day.

Mrs. Spencer also has the students monitor whether they have followed the rules each day. She decides that there isn't enough time in the day to do the monitoring periodically throughout the day, so she has the students wait until the end of the day to monitor the rules as well as the goals. Again activities get rushed at the end of the day, and, at least three of five days each week, she just doesn't get to the goal review, and rule monitoring also gets postponed.

What was wrong with Mrs. Spencer's use of these two self-management techniques? First of all, Mrs. Spencer does not model how to write a daily goal — she doesn't think it is important for her to establish a goal. Educators must remember that they are role models for their students, and waiting to monitor the students' goals and following rules until the end of the day is too long of a period of time when first starting a project. Intervals need to be shorter so that the students

143

can see success and have the opportunity for more positive reinforcement. In all classrooms, activities get rushed at the end of the day; however, it is important to set priorities. The students learn how much the teacher values these activities by whether he/she makes time to do them. If the students think that the teacher does not consider the activity important, it will not be important to the student either.

Definition of Self-Management Techniques

Self-management is the application of behavior-change processes to modify or maintain one's own behavior. It empowers students to be independent performers (Johns, Crowley and Guetzloe 2002). Teaching students to establish goals for themselves gives students the power to control their own day. Teaching students to monitor whether they follow the rules of the classroom provides students the opportunity to analyze and reflect on their own behavior. In the real world, many individuals do not have goals. One early study showed that only 10 percent of the people have goals and only 3 percent of individuals have written goals. Individuals who do have written goals accomplish 50 to 100 times more than the others (Mitchell and McCollum 1987). It is critical that, at an early age, we teach children to set realistic goals, write those goals down, and reflect on whether the goals were reached or not and the reason they were or were not reached.

In establishing goals for themselves, students should be taught to either write a behavioral or an academic goal for themselves for the day; what they want to accomplish in either area.

When teaching students to monitor their own success in following the classroom rules, the educator is moving from exhibiting his/her control of the student's behavior to the student determining whether he or she is controlling behavior. The educator is teaching the student to monitor and evaluate his or her own behavior.

Correct Use of Self-Management

The advantages of using self-management techniques are many, if the techniques are utilized appropriately. Kaplan and Carter (1995) found that self-management strategies can be effective in changing academic and social behavior. Students who can manage themselves save teacher time and energy. While the initial work for the teacher may be labor-intensive, the long-term benefits will be reaped by both educators and students. Self-management ability on the part of the student can lead to increased generalization to other areas and to high maintenance of the behavior, which is an important goal.

When beginning the process of goal setting it is critical that the teacher works with the students to focus on one goal for the day. There also must be several opportunities throughout the day to monitor whether the student is achieving his/her goal. The frequency of the monitoring can then slowly be decreased according to the progress the students are making. After students become familiar and skilled at the process, some teachers then work with their students to establish two or three goals for the week, and the students review their progress on the goals daily with the culminating reflection on whether the goals were met occurring at the end of the week. As in the example of how Mrs. Wilson utilized goal setting, she modeled the behavior by sharing with her students her own goal for the day. She also shared with her students her progress in meeting her goal.

Students should post their goals and their progress on following rules. Having a visual reminder increases the likelihood that the student will meet the goal(s) and will follow the rules.

When students are establishing their own goals, they are involved in a non-competitive activity that fosters their individual growth. They also are involved in an activity where one student may help another student meet his/her goal. That action can then be reinforced by the teacher. Unlike in a competitive activity, students don't work for each other, instead they are working for themselves, and to "win." In a goal-setting activity, all students can be a winner and can learn the value of caring for other individual classmates.

When first implementing this intervention, teachers should provide frequent opportunities for students to monitor whether they have followed the rules. For young children, monitoring should occur about every 5-10 minutes. It also is critical that rules be kept to a minimum — four to five is an ideal number with which to begin. All rules should be stated positively, and students should be taught the meaning of the rules. As an example, a rule might be: Raise your hand before speaking. For young children, there should be a visual depiction of the rule — perhaps a picture of a child raising his hand. An example of a set of rules that would need to be taught might be: Respect others, respect self, and respect property. With these particular rules, the teacher should teach what each phrase means — to respect others may mean remaining quiet when someone else is speaking, saying kind words to others, providing praise to others, keeping hands to self, etc.

The educator should provide frequent positive feedback and reinforcement to the students who are following the rules. And there should be a system in place whereas the teacher can let the students know whether or not she agrees with their self-assessment that they have followed the rules. When there is an occasion where the student notes that he followed the rule, yet the teacher observed otherwise, the teacher has an obligation to point this out to the student in a respectful manner. She should approach the student with whom she does not agree and request quietly that the student take a look at his/her analysis again while pointing out the specific behaviors she observed. She then should provide encouragement to the student that he or she can follow the rule during the next period of time. As an example, the teacher might say quietly to the student: "Jim, I know that you are trying to remember to raise your hand to ask a question, but remember that you did make a statement without doing so. Look at that again and let's try to get a checkmark next period." If the student erases the checkmark, the teacher should thank the student and move on. Generally it will be very rare when this does occur. Students usually are harder on themselves when self-evaluating their own performance than the adult may be. Students who are honest in their analysis should be reinforced for evaluating the behavior correctly.

Cautions in the Use of Self-Management

1. As seen in the example of how Mrs. Jones made mistakes in the use of goal setting and monitoring of the rules, the teacher must be a role model for the students and also engage in goal-setting.

2. If the teacher determines that he or she will utilize these two self-management techniques, then it will be necessary to allot time to engage in the activities. These must be a priority within the classroom. Every time the teacher doesn't get to a specific activity, the students may view it as a message that the activity is not important.

3. It is critical that the teacher start out with small steps in the use of these two particular self-management techniques. In the beginning, it is too long to wait to review the goal or review the rule-following until the end of the day. Students will need more immediate feedback in order to be successful. If they see success after a short period of time, then success breeds success and the student is more likely to continue to be successful.

As Armstrong (1999) stated, ". . . it may be far better to use behavioral strategies that *internally empower* students than those that externally control them." (p. 97).

References

Armstrong, T. (1999). *ADD/ADHD alternatives in the classroom.* Alexandria, VA: Association for Supervision and Curriculum Development.

Johns, B., Crowley, E., and Guetzloe, E. (2002). *Effective curriculum for students with emotional and behavioral disorders.* Denver: Love Publishing.

Kaplan, J., and Carter, J. (1995). *Beyond behavior modification: a cognitive-behavioral approach to behavior management in the schools.* Austin, Texas: Pro-Ed.

Mitchell, M. and McCollum, M. (1987). *Learning to be positive.* Birmingham, AL; EBSCO Media.

Conclusion

As more students with behavioral challenges enter our school doors, it is critical that we utilize appropriate and effective interventions to meet their needs and to assure their educational and social success. Educators must be proactive and positive in their efforts to deter behavioral problems. There is no "one-size-fits-all" approach to behavior management. This book presented scenarios that demonstrated that point and offered several interventions that you can use to help control inappropriate behavioral challenges in the classroom and interventions that suggest techniques for eliciting and managing appropriate behaviors from your students. This book has also provided you with practical advice on the correct use of each intervention so that the integrity of each of these behavioral interventions is maintained. Our goal must be to successfully keep children within our schools and to meet their needs through the appropriate use of behavioral interventions.